<RE
BOOT
ING/
TECH
CULTURE:

<RE BOOT ING/ TECH CULTURE:

How to Ignite Innovation and Build Organizations Where Everyone Can Thrive

<by> TELLE WHITNEY

HARVARD BUSINESS REVIEW PRESS
BOSTON, MASSACHUSETTS

The web addresses referenced in this book were live and correct at the time of the book's publication but may be subject to change.

Library of Congress Cataloging-in-Publication Data

Names: Whitney, Telle, author.
Title: Rebooting tech culture : how to ignite innovation and build organizations where everyone can thrive / Telle Whitney.
Description: Boston, Massachusetts : Harvard Business Review Press, [2025] | Includes index.
Identifiers: LCCN 2024045943 (print) | LCCN 2024045944 (ebook) | ISBN 9781647829858 (hardcover) | ISBN 9781647829865 (epub)
Subjects: LCSH: High technology industries—Management. | Leadership. | Industrial management. | Diversity in the workplace.
Classification: LCC HD62.37 .W49 2025 (print) | LCC HD62.37 (ebook) | DDC 658—dc23/eng/20250131
LC record available at https://lccn.loc.gov/2024045943
LC ebook record available at https://lccn.loc.gov/2024045944

ISBN: 978-1-64782-985-8
eISBN: 978-1-64782-986-5

The paper used in this publication meets the requirements of the American National Standard for Permanence of Paper for Publications and Documents in Libraries and Archives Z39.48-1992.

To my dear friend and fellow troublemaker Anita Borg.
Your partnership and our friendship changed my world
and is the inspiration for this book.

CONTENTS

<RE BOOT ING/ TECH CULTURE:

< **INTRODUCTION** >

An inclusive environment is the best environment
for building great things. It forces you into a set
of habits that let you get the best out of all
the members of the team.

**—Kevin Scott, CTO, Microsoft;
former CTO, LinkedIn**

I n 1986, having just earned my PhD in computer science at the California Institute of Technology, I arrived in Silicon Valley. The '80s were a time of massive innovation. Tech company after tech company—from Sun Microsystems to Cisco to Silicon Graphics—was being founded, creating products that had not been possible without the computing power delivered by the wide availability of increasingly complex chips. I could not wait to take part in this technology revolution.

After a short stint in a research lab, I joined Actel, a startup that designed and manufactured field-programmable gate arrays. The technology was new and exciting, providing the ability to implement an application-specific design in any lab, using proprietary methods. I loved it. Over the next few years I would lead the development of design software, programmable processors, and a voice-over IP processor—all of which were groundbreaking.

Fueled by a passion for creating innovative products, I climbed the ladder at Actel and another startup called Malleable Technologies, where I became vice president of engineering. Often I was the only woman in the room, especially in product and engineering discussions.

All the technological innovations we enjoy today grew out of the ideas from those early days of Silicon Valley. The Mead and Conway revolution—the method for very large-scale integration (VLSI) design—was built on Moore's Law, the observation by Gordon Moore, cofounder of Intel, that the number of transistors on a chip would double every two years.[1] As compute power doubled and tripled, an army of entrepreneurs applied it to many technical problems, leading to radically new solutions. Engineers, including me, developed chip modules based on standardized design rules that could be used in many contexts, creating the foundation for application-specific designs. The meaning that this work held for me—the desire to be part of a movement that can change the world—was and continues to be my attraction to technology.

Over the years, I have had the opportunity to meet people from wildly different backgrounds—engineers, software developers, and product managers of varying genders, races, nationalities, physical abilities, and economic statuses—all of whom had the same fire in their eyes as I did when Silicon Valley captured my imagination. They, too, have seen the promise of technology and want to be part of its future. They, too, want to change the world.

Li Fan was born in China and was in graduate school when she decided to accept a full-time position in Silicon Valley. She loved the diverse community of the area. She eventually rose to senior engineering leadership roles at Pinterest, Lime, and Google. Seeing the impact of her efforts was important to Fan. "Google gave me a sense of fulfillment that every time I implemented something and launched a new feature, millions of users used it immediately," she told me. "There were bugs and crashes, and I felt their pain, but it was a joy to see the result of my work."

Mary Lou Jepsen, cofounder and CEO of Openwater, a startup focused on revolutionizing patient care, was the first chief technology officer (CTO) of One Laptop per Child, a nonprofit that aimed to bring educational devices to children around the world. When she first connected with Nicholas Negroponte, the nonprofit's founder, at the MIT Media Lab to talk about the initiative, they were supposed to meet for five minutes. It turned into six hours. Their shared enthusiasm for the social impact of the startup was clear from the beginning. "The project scaled quickly, and there were a hundred thousand people working on our project," she explained. "What was important was to transform the opportunity for kids in the developing world with little or no educational opportunity."

But while I've seen the fire shine brightly in the eyes of technologists like Fan and Jepsen, more often than not I've watched it disappear from the eyes of so many people from underrepresented groups. Many of them still experience an exclusionary culture similar to the one that was prevalent in my early years. When you are the *only one* in the room—the only female engineer, the only Black technical lead, the only nonbinary or LGBTQ+ software developer, the only data analyst who uses a wheelchair—and are made to feel that you don't belong in technology's white and Asian male–dominated culture, the fire gets extinguished. The desire to pursue your passions is snuffed out of you. Imagine joining an organization where the leadership has taken great pains to hire you because of your expertise. Then you experience meeting after meeting where your male or white (or both) colleagues talk over you, ignore you, or discuss privately whether you were hired only because you belong to an underrepresented group. Then you meet with your manager, who seems rather uncomfortable speaking to you and seems to think you aren't capable of taking on projects that in reality match your skills. Why would you stay?

Facing these kinds of obstacles, some people move into positions or departments that are more welcoming. But too many leave tech for a different career. Gaby Aguilera, who worked at Google but quit technology to become a medical doctor, is one of them. Ellora Israni, who at Stanford University cofounded she++, a nonprofit that encourages women to pursue technology, is another.[2] Israni originally went into computer science because, as she explained, "I thought it was a way to do useful things for the world." But soon she grew tired of being one of the few women in the room and dispirited by the lack of Black and Latine technologists in her team. She eventually left the technology field to become a lawyer.

I'm not saying anything is wrong with these talented women finding a new path. A lawyer working on social justice and a medical doctor helping people are clear assets to our world. But Israni and Aguilera are part of a pattern I've observed: young, talented people from underrepresented groups trying to make a career in technology, then leaving the field behind. The rigors of being an *only* in an unwelcoming workplace culture—being both dismissed and scrutinized, feeling unable to bring their whole selves to work but holding back to fit in, experiencing loneliness—eventually made the technology field less tolerable, and they found other options.

I also know that technology and its impact on our lives is profound. Today, it is ubiquitous in our world, from personal devices to the search and online tools we use daily to the AI already embedded in our systems. Tomorrow, it will be present in every medical conversation we have and will advise us on every decision we make through smart homes, electronic vehicles, and other AI systems we'll be connected to. We have already seen what happens when products are not developed by diverse teams: they don't work for everyone—or, worse, discriminate against groups of people. Think of crash car dummies that don't represent women's bodies, leading to vehicle designs that cause more injuries for female passengers; AI-powered recruitment tools that have built-in biases against racially diverse candidates; health-monitoring apps that track everything from blood pressure to calories burned, but not a woman's period; voice recognition systems that don't recognize women's voices; and so many more.[3] The generative AI tools being widely used in 2025 rely on a massive amount of data from the internet that bakes in our prejudices as they predict and encourage future solutions. The potential for an increasingly biased future is horrifying.

There is no question that the world is better when people like Israni and Aguilera are engaged in technology creation. Innovative products benefit from having engineers of all backgrounds work on them. In the late nineties Lynn Conway, a partner in the Mead and Conway VLSI revolution, came out as transgender, which deeply inspired me and impacted my life. Her contributions to system design and scalable design rules were critical to the entire chip revolution. Diversity of thought has been demonstrated, time after time, to be essential for developing truly new ideas.

Slow Progress

Today, I'm no longer working as a technologist. For over twenty years I channeled my passion into new kinds of chips and the exciting products that they enabled. But I became increasingly interested in ensuring more women sit at the table when technologies are being developed. In 1994, tired of attending conferences where there were only men, Anita Borg—a fellow computer scientist and close friend—and I founded the Grace Hopper

Celebration of Women in Computing. The conference now attracts more than thirty thousand attendees, mostly women who want to learn about new technologies, hone their skills, network, find jobs, and support one another.

In 2002 I took over the helm of the Institute for Women and Technology, which Anita had founded in 1997. My dear friend was dying, and the nonprofit was still in an early and ill-defined state, so I accepted the CEO role. Over the next fifteen years I would build the organization—later renamed the Anita Borg Institute for Women and Technology, and now called AnitaB.org—into what it is today. I channeled my passion for the world-changing potential of technology to help create conferences and leadership workshops for women from many racial and ethnic backgrounds who were considering a technology career; successful women working in tech; and faculty, academic, and technology leaders committed to creating inclusive cultures. I also had the opportunity to work closely with key executives from what are now industry behemoths, like Google, Meta, Amazon, and Microsoft, and listened to thousands of women who joined these organizations. Then and now, all I've wanted is for *all* people in technology to thrive.

But there's still much to do.

Decades after being one of the few women PhD students in my department at Caltech, I still meet male engineers who believe the field is a zero-sum game: if more women are working in technology jobs and being promoted, their thinking goes, then men lose. These engineers fight their managers about diversity and inclusion goals because *they* feel excluded. In 2023 a large contingent of men showed up for the recruiting fair at the Grace Hopper Celebration. Men have always been welcome at the conference, but its focus has centered on increasing *women's* participation in computing, and the male engineers who attend have usually demonstrated appreciation for that goal. The job market has changed, though, and that year some men, feeling excluded from the large and effective recruiting process that has become part of the Grace Hopper conference experience, showed up in large numbers. According to news coverage, "Videos posted to social media showed scenes of men flocking around recruiters, running into event venues, and cutting in front of women to get an interview slot."[4]

It's no wonder that despite their promises of change, many technology leaders treat efforts like sensitivity training and diversity, equity, and inclusion (DEI) initiatives merely as boxes to be checked. They want to *talk* about these efforts—they want to talk about all the small tweaks they've made to their processes—but they do not want to change.

Don't get me wrong: there is great benefit in launching programs like unconscious bias and sensitivity training, as well as DEI initiatives like targeted leadership development, novel hiring practices, and affinity groups. (And there are many books, articles, and organizations that can help you do just that.) However, their impact will always be limited if an organization doesn't have a culture that values everyone's perspectives.

If your technical culture is not set up to appreciate and value all employees, what they bring to the table and why they matter, then—at best—many of your managers and technical leads will react to DEI programs with apathy. They'll think of them as troublesome bureaucratic processes they must work around. At worst, they will resist, fight, or unwittingly undermine these programs. And when employees from underrepresented groups who were hired simply to meet company goals—and whom their colleagues don't truly welcome into their communities—leave, it will be used as evidence that inclusivity is not a worthwhile strategy.

No, tweaks won't do. Change is only possible when you change the *whole* culture.

The Power of the Six Cs

While I was CEO of the Anita Borg Institute, I learned a great deal about what works to make tech cultures welcoming to underrepresented groups. I've found that the very values that fuel a culture of innovation are also at the heart of organizations that support talent from all walks of life. Doing so requires taking coordinated actions that are designed to fundamentally change your culture and foster one that nurtures what I call the six Cs:

- **Creativity.** All employees are encouraged to bring their unique perspectives and to collaborate to innovate. Creativity is, of course, the core of a culture of innovation. Generating original solutions requires developing all your employees so they can work together effectively.

- **Courage.** All employees are encouraged to take risks. Courage is critical to creativity and innovation; you can develop novel solutions and products only if you are willing to try new things. Technical managers, too, must take what may feel like risks when it comes to their people, including hiring employees from a variety of backgrounds, fighting preconceived notions of what staff with different skill sets and experiences bring to the table, and giving high-risk, high-reward assignments to all high-potential employees.

- **Confidence.** All employees are encouraged to believe in their ability to succeed or accomplish a specific task. Leaders who develop confidence in their staff create a culture where ideas are confidently expressed during brainstorming discussions, and where feedback is given freely and respectfully—not hidden. In such cultures, advocates or sponsors for all employees are part of the cultural DNA.

- **Curiosity.** All employees are invited to ask questions, challenge assumptions, and learn from diverse and multidisciplinary perspectives. Curiosity leads technologists to devise new ways of approaching problems and meeting market demands. It also helps them be open to new ideas about what talent looks like and to fight "not the way we do things here" attitudes.

- **Communication.** All employees are able to contribute in meetings regularly, and *everyone* has a chance to present their technical ideas. Communication is not just about speaking up—it's also about listening. Organizations that nurture clear communication encourage technical leads and managers to deliver clear feedback and effectively navigate difficult conversations, including those about gender and racial biases and discrimination present in the organization.

- **Community.** All employees feel they belong. Community is the soil where great ideas are born, grown, and nurtured. Creating it within an organization, and helping employees plug into external communities, allows technology innovation and people alike to flourish.

This book is about how these six Cs can power real change in your organization, helping you create a place where innovation thrives *and* employees of any background can succeed and contribute. With the attention and commitment of technology leaders, we can systematically create cultures of innovation *and* inclusion.

In each chapter, I'll dig deeper into one of the Cs and share examples from leaders who have made a meaningful change at the companies they work (or worked) for—including Microsoft, Google, Facebook, LinkedIn, Intel, IBM, AMD, and Redfin. At the end of every chapter, I'll provide actions you can take to cultivate the six Cs in your organization.

To better understand what has truly worked to create tech cultures that are innovative and welcoming, I interviewed forty-six people, thirty-four of whom are tech executives and CTOs with experience at startups, midsize organizations, and large, leading companies. Of these executives, 47 percent are men and 53 percent are women. In terms of their racial or ethnic backgrounds, the group is 56 percent white, 21 percent Asian, 15 percent Black, and 9 percent Latine. I also interviewed twelve young women engineers—33 percent white, 25 percent Black, 25 percent Latine, and 17 percent Asian.

Partnering with a social science researcher from UCLA's Momentum, an institute dedicated to researching gender equality in tech, I created a survey—one of the few of its kind—that sought to understand the experiences of tech employees of all genders and backgrounds. With the help of organizations such as Systers (an electronic mailing list for women in computing), DiscoverE (an organization dedicated to engaging students in engineering careers), the Center for Minorities and People with Disabilities in Information Technology, Mocha Moms (a community of Black mothers), and IEEE (the world's largest technical professional organization), I was able to collect more than one thousand responses from people in a wide range of companies and technical fields. I'll share some of their anonymous stories.

As you read about the six Cs, keep in mind that they don't constitute a step-by-step program. You have to be aware of all the Cs and work on them in a concerted effort—they are deeply intertwined. Together, they are clarifying lenses that allow you to see anew and rethink your approaches to how you create a sense of belonging and innovation in your organization.

We Need You

The stories from my interviews and survey will, I hope, show why we *must* speed up the pace of change across the entire technology industry. It might be tempting to think of the exclusionary nature of tech cultures as a "niche concern," especially in the face of the many challenges facing the industry. As I write this, giants like Google, Microsoft, Salesforce, and Meta have announced and are rolling out tens of thousands of layoffs; startups are struggling to find funding following the increase of interest rates; and large language models such as OpenAI's ChatGPT, Microsoft Copilot, and Google Gemini are making headlines for both providing massive opportunities for novel products and uses and raising ethical red flags.

But the need to diversify our technical workforce has never been more urgent. As slow as progress has been for women and people of color, the pandemic and Great Resignation may have had a lasting negative effect. In 2018, women left technical jobs at a rate of 6.1 percent.[5] That rate more than doubled for women to 16 percent in 2022 and increased even more for Black women (25 percent).[6] Confronted by the challenge of balancing home and childcare responsibilities with demanding roles in unsupportive environments, many technical women and people of color have left. Although in 2023 the attrition rate for women decreased to 13.5 percent, it was still significantly higher than it was five years before.[7] Ignoring this stubborn problem will have severe consequences for the future of responsible innovation.

Culture change is not a comfortable topic. When you set out to create it, you must be honest about your organization's flaws and accept and listen to feedback. This book is for technology leaders, from middle managers to CTOs, of organizations of all sizes—and even those not traditionally considered to be in the tech industry. Whether you lead a large division or a single department, *you* have the ability to create or evolve your group's culture by fostering the six Cs. Whether you work in a US company or one of the countless technology organizations across the world, *you* can unleash innovation and make sure everyone is welcome. Diversity and representation often look different from country to country. The factors that impact women working in technology in India at either local or foreign-based companies, for example, may be quite different from those that affect women in the United States. But inclusion is critical *everywhere*. If your organization employs people who are consistently "othered," then this book is for you. You might need to tailor the advice to your context, but you have the power to leverage the six Cs to create a better culture.

The fact is, we need you. You are a gatekeeper of your organization. Only when you become our ally will we be able to create highly innovative companies where anyone can thrive.

The book highlights many such allies in the tech world who are committed to creating better cultures. While their stories are centered on the work they did prior to the publication of this book, it's important to recognize that individual companies' cultures ebb and flow over time. People leave; leadership changes hands; cultures are transformed and then revert back. These companies may behave very differently today—and not always for the better.

In fact, since 2023 a backlash against the very concept of diversity and inclusion has been growing. DEI efforts have come under attack from lawmakers in Florida, Utah, and Texas, among other states, and from white billionaires like Elon Musk and Bill

Ackman.[8] The Israel-Hamas war has created political tension on college campuses and divisive arguments in the employee chat rooms of companies like Google and X, raising even more questions about the future of DEI.[9] Responding to this backlash, some of the companies whose inclusive practices are featured in this book are now backpedaling. According to an article in *Fast Company,* "A recent CNBC report . . . revealed that some organizations in 2023 were scaling back their commitment to these values, evidenced by layoffs of DEI staff, reductions in support for diverse employee resource groups, curtailed learning and development initiatives, and drastic budget cuts—up to 90 percent in some cases—for external DEI groups."[10]

More than ever, we need technology leaders—we need you—to recommit to making our organizations places where anyone can contribute their best ideas to create the breakthrough technologies that transform our lives. Fostering the six Cs is a good place to start.

A Note to Readers

Just as the landscape of DEI is changing, so is the language used to describe groups that have been historically underrepresented in the workplace. This language will continue to evolve as we continue to grapple with which terms are most useful and acceptable to those they describe. While labels can be problematic, they are sometimes necessary. In this book, I use the terms Black, Latine, Asian, Indigenous, LGBTQ+, and people with disabilities to describe some of the groups who have been, and still are, underrepresented in tech cultures. I've chosen to use the term Latine generally, unless I'm referring specifically to someone who self-identifies as Latina or Latino. To list each of these groups separately in every instance I refer to them collectively would be repetitive and slow to read. To that end, I've chosen the term "underrepresented groups" to describe them.

Over the course of my career as a white woman in the technology arena, I have continued to learn about how many people face overlapping challenges due to multiple aspects of their identities, a concept often referred to as intersectionality.[11] Since I joined the field, there has been measurable progress in women's participation, although there is still more work to do. But for many groups progress is often slow, and their numbers are still small. I hope this book can help all of us change that.

‹ 1 ›
TECH'S CULTURE PROBLEM

If you don't have the courage to shine a light on the things you're doing wrong, you'll never correct them.

—Blake Irving, former CEO, GoDaddy

From its early days, the Silicon Valley tech culture, rooted in the 1960s counterculture, has aspired to a utopian vision in which computing and creativity can change the world for the good.[1] In the early 2000s this vision was best expressed by Google's (now former) motto, "Don't be evil."[2] Yet in 2025 it is clear that much of big tech has not lived up to its utopian dreams. Over the past decade, the industry has been rocked by scandal after scandal, revealing an underlying culture of discrimination, sexual harassment, and biased behavior that is fundamentally unwelcoming to women and people of color. People of all genders and backgrounds who have been affected by this exclusionary culture have started to go public, a difficult decision that dramatically impacts their lives.

In 2017 Susan Fowler, then a twenty-five-year-old engineer, penned an explosive blog post shining a light on Uber's frat-boy, sexist culture and the treatment she and other women endured there.[3] She wrote about being propositioned by her manager on her first day; about other women reporting the same manager for inappropriate behavior and receiving no HR support; about sexist behavior and biased performance reviews that hindered her advancement; and about explicit retaliation for reporting all of this that was ignored by management.

In 2020 Françoise Brougher won $22.5 million from Pinterest after going public about being fired.[4] According to the *New York Times*, she "had been left out of important meetings, was given gendered feedback, was paid less than her male peers when she joined the company, and ultimately was let go for speaking up about it." Brougher shared her story because she believed it *should* be told.

In 2020 Dr. Timnit Gebru was fired from her role as technical co-lead of the Ethical Artificial Intelligence Team at Google for coauthoring a paper that discussed bias in AI models and for sending emails to leadership about diversity problems at the company. Her termination fueled a Twitter storm of condemnation for Google, with three thousand employees and four thousand academics signing a letter protesting her firing.[5]

April Christina Curley, a Black queer woman who had led the recruitment of engineers from historically Black colleges and universities (HBCUs) at Google, was also fired in 2020. Her allegations of racial bias in the hiring and recruitment of Black and Latine graduates from HBCUs were met with anger in online media.[6]

Whenever stories like these illuminate the sexism and racism that plague tech companies, the companies often respond defensively with short-term diversity and inclusion plans. They implement sexual harassment training across the organization and vow to boost the number of women and people of color they will hire and promote into leadership roles. They invest millions of dollars in programs and initiatives they believe or have been told will attract talent from all backgrounds and sustain diversity in their organizations. They create affinity groups for employees from underrepresented groups, host women-led conferences, and sponsor outside programs such as K–12 education to address the so-called "pipeline issue."

But at least six years after many of these investments were made by leading tech companies, including Google, Meta, and Amazon, the lack of progress is obvious to anyone who looks at the data. Today a significant number of employees in technology roles continue to be white men, while Black, Latine, and Indigenous populations are still greatly underrepresented. LGBTQ+ people and people with disabilities are also few in number, but most organizations do not track them. And although there are many Asian engineers, they are sorely missing in leadership, especially women. I've listened to HR and diversity leaders proudly describe the programs they support—including unconscious bias training, employee resource groups, mentorship programs, you name it—only to review their data and find very little year-over-year change for these groups, particularly at the senior and executive levels.

According to AnitaB.org's 2023 Top Company report, women in technical roles increased in aggregate from 26.2 percent in 2019 to 29 percent in 2023, with the most significant increase occurring at the entry level (growing from 33.1 percent to 35.5 percent). The number of people of color in technical roles is much more dismal, with the report showing 6.1 percent Black employees and 6.6 percent Latine; the only group with a more substantial presence in technical roles is Asians: 28 percent.[7]

These numbers don't quite add up when compared with the computer science graduation rates of individuals from these groups. According to the National Center for Women and Information Technology (NCWIT), in 2023, 24 percent of computer science and information science undergraduates were women; of the graduates from those programs, 12 percent were Latine, 8 percent were Black, 19 percent were Asian, and 4 percent were multiracial.[8]

The lack of progress companies have made in diversifying their technological roles is baffling, given that the business case for diverse and inclusive cultures is well established. As far back as 2018, McKinsey's "Delivering through Diversity" report showed that companies in the top quartile for gender, ethnic, and racial diversity were more likely to have financial returns above the industry mean.[9] But the business case is not just about financial returns—diverse teams also perform better. An NCWIT study on patents, for example, showed that mixed-gender teams produce the most highly cited patents.[10] Other research has repeatedly demonstrated that teams with diverse perspectives produce more solutions, especially for hard problems. And as someone who's devoted a large part of her career to developing innovations, it's clear to me that the impact and usefulness of new technologies and products improve significantly when diverse teams create them.

Most business leaders do not doubt the value of an inclusive culture. I have encountered countless senior technical leaders who support the idea of having more people of underrepresented groups in technical and leadership positions in their organizations. They champion many of the programs designed to hire and retain these employees. So why has there been so little progress?

Because these same leaders pay lip service to diversity but don't make it a core principle in their decision-making. For example, the head of engineering talks about the importance of hiring women but doesn't promote any women into his leadership team. A CEO never fails to mention DEI in all-hands meetings but rarely reviews the data on inclusion with his executive team and hires a diversity officer who reports to HR instead of him. An HR leader, tasked with improving the retention of Black tech workers, sets up an employee resource group for them but doesn't fund it, leaving volunteer members to run it with little support.

The hard truth is that most leaders don't want to fundamentally change their workplaces. As one well-known technology leader told me, "I don't want to change our culture; it works great for us! I just want more women."

Yes, that culture works great—for *you*. But it's obviously not working for women in your organization, and it is especially not working for tech people of color, those with disabilities, or those who identify as LGBTQ+. That's because the classic culture of a tech organization, department, or team is rooted in two myths and one obsession—and all three lead to exclusionary behavior.

Two Myths and One Obsession

When people think about the tech industry, they often think about companies like Google, Meta, Apple, Amazon, and Cisco, among others. These are the behemoths whose tech products and services impact our lives.

But the industry is not monolithic. Many, if not most, technology organizations are midsize, and many are not even traditional technology companies. Redfin, for example, might be a real estate company, but its tech division is instrumental to its success, and the CEO and CTO know it. Additionally, every bank includes a large and sophisticated technology group that creates its tech products. As AI becomes increasingly important, many banks and insurance companies see these in-house groups as the secret sauce of their future. The fact is that today, all companies both in the United States and around the globe are tech companies. While tech organizations exist in many sizes and forms, however, their cultures can be surprisingly similar because they are often born of two myths and one obsession.

The first myth is a narrow ideal of what a great technology employee or leader looks and acts like: male, hypercompetitive, willing to work long hours (especially late nights and weekends), well-versed in geek esoterica, and a natural-born genius who graduated from one of a few elite computer science programs. Consciously or unconsciously, managers underestimate, under-challenge, and overlook those who deviate from this ideal, regard-less of their actual technical skills or potential. Conversely, those who conform to it are often *over*valued and rewarded with more opportunities that help them grow and showcase their skills, fuel-ing a self-fulfilling prophecy.

The second myth is meritocracy—the fierce belief, especially propagated by the utopian dream of Silicon Valley, that talent, ideas, and pitches for potential companies are evaluated strictly on merit. I have heard industry icons proudly espouse their be-lief in meritocracy and its power to overcome bias. But find any-one who does not match the ideal of a talented tech person, and ask them if Silicon Valley truly runs on merit—most will laugh outright.

Emily Chang does an outstanding job of describing the myth of meritocracy in her book *Brotopia*, an enlightening examination of how it has led tech to its current exclusionary culture.[11] She ex-plains that, while many Silicon Valley companies were "devoted to the idea of meritocracy—of hiring only the best—that is simply not what happened." Instead, engineers who founded companies or rose up the ranks brought people just like them on board. One of the members of the "PayPal mafia"—a group of former PayPal employees, including Reid Hoffman, Elon Musk, and Peter Thiel, who have gone on to found many other tech companies—admitted to "wanting to employ people who were a lot like them."

My experience with the Silicon Valley ethos of meritocracy is that this focus on recruiting people who are "just like me" and who fit the ideal of a tech worker is representative of how many organizations fill their ranks. Whether they realize it or not, leaders and managers gravitate toward and hire people who meet their narrow subjective criteria. These decision-makers have achieved a measure of success, so they unconsciously assume that others who have backgrounds and experiences similar to their own must also be great. They conflate the ideal of a great tech employee (which they themselves often fit) with actual, demonstrated competence and talent.[12] Meritocracy has nothing to do with their approach.

I believe there's nothing wrong with valuing technical talent. The problem is that the two myths conspire to ensure the potential and contributions of some individuals—especially those who don't fit the narrow ideal—don't have much of a chance to develop and shine.

The exclusionary nature of these two myths is amplified by engineers' and software developers' obsession with "geniuses." The idea that all great innovations spring from the minds of gifted loners, not the creative collaboration of many people, has been around for more than three hundred years, since gaining momentum in the 1700s.[13] In tech cultures, this (now debunked) belief has endured in the often cult-like reverence for technical leaders such as rock-star developers who "can do the work of ten regular ones."[14] Their technical prowess and contributions are perceived as being so valuable that top management and HR protect them at all costs. This often means ignoring or excusing any inappropriate behavior as "eccentric" rather than calling it what it often is: exclusionary. For example, a young woman told me that a technical lead at her company did not talk to female engineers—as a matter of principle. Everyone accepted his behavior because he was deemed critical to the technical team: *Well, you know him—he's odd but a genius. Whatever keeps him happy . . .* Sometimes even egregious behavior, such as subjecting others to racist remarks or harassing female engineers, is excused if the perpetrator is a highly valued employee.

Such blatantly exclusionary behavior might be rare. But it is *not* uncommon for technical work environments—from startups to global behemoths to tech departments inside every company— to feel hostile to people from underrepresented groups. With no chance for them to look like or fit the idealized version of a great worker, or to meet narrow, biased-from-the-start criteria for success in a field that glorifies individual genius and excuses bad behavior, the stage is set for technologists of underrepresented groups to be excluded.

An Unfair Playing Field for "Onlys"

For far too many tech employees who find themselves the "only" in the room—the only one who is female, Black, Latine, LGBTQ+, or a person with disabilities, for example—work is a place to endure endless microaggressions and engage in constant code-switching. Outright sexist, racist, homophobic, and ableist jokes and slurs may be less common today in tech workplaces, but they've often been replaced by equally discriminatory and hurtful behavior, like male employees casually calling women "girls" or saying the company lowers its hiring standard for Black or Latine candidates. Recently, a student I met told me she was hired by one of the big tech companies, and before she started, some of her new male colleagues told her she only got the job because she was a woman. She is not alone.

In the survey I conducted for this book, many technologists—mostly women—who identified as members of underrepresented groups shared stories of being devalued, discriminated against, and discouraged at work. Here are some of their comments:

> "I didn't get big projects because there was a perception that I couldn't work late because I picked my kids up from school."
>   —**Black woman, business analyst and technical coach**

> "Being the only female at the manager or higher level of an organization was terrible. I was treated differently and disrespected by my peers, my leaders, as well as staff. The discrimination and harassment were often subtle, but they were everywhere. Given the highly unbalanced gender divide, it was impossible to stand up or point out the problems. Any attempts were dismissed as [me being] overly sensitive."
>   —**White woman, engineer**

> "In [a] job I had in technology, [I was] accused of sleeping with male supervisors because they were sponsoring my career and mentoring me. The owners decided that I was not smart enough to be in my field and that I was hired solely because I was an attractive Latina woman."
>   —**Latina, computer/system analyst**

> "My year-end write-up stated that I no longer demonstrated company values because of my sexual identity."
>   —**Indigenous woman, systems security engineer**

> "My opinion is often ignored, and I am often left out of important meetings and discussions."
>   —**White woman, fellow/tech lead**

"My manager constantly belittled me by trying to assign admin, junior-related tasks to me. Death from a thousand paper cuts."

    —Asian woman, chief technology officer

"Fellow first-level managers . . . would question my proposed improvements, and then would slightly modify and present them as their own. Those who opposed my recommendations would support the updated version of my proposal."

    —Latina, mechanical engineer

"My age and my gender constantly worked against me. I was never good enough. I was always too young, even when doing a vast majority of the work. My intern was hired as a senior engineer because I advocated we hire him. My promotion was denied because he was getting married and starting a family, so I 'didn't need it' like he did."

    —White woman, software engineer

"Almost every new team [I've been asked to move into] has required that I work with male baby boomer colleagues who have been hostile about being led by me, a much younger woman of color (as a day-to-day engineering lead, not a manager). What I've experienced so far . . . at two different companies is [a willingness] to acknowledge the obstacles, but NOT for superiors to speak to their difficult employees about correcting their behavior, either because they feel it will not change anything or they feel the employee has a personal excuse that explains their behavior."

    —Asian woman, material process engineer

"I know that I have consistently been paid approximately $20,000 less than men with less training doing easier jobs. One example: I was the only woman in the IT architect series in a job where I supervised eleven people. I made the same amount as men who were individual contributors. Probably worst, though, was that when policy was being made, I was often totally excluded in favor of white men with little or no real background or training in IT—that really hurt."

    —White woman, fellow/tech lead

"In my previous company, it was a lot of tech bro culture. People with kids were considered bad engineers since they can't be on call all the time. There was a lot of explicit gender stereotyping happening across the company."

    —Asian woman, software/engineering tech lead/fellow

"I was CTO of [a startup]. The male staff reports were always pushing their way over my lead, but mostly in subtle ways that were difficult to call out, resulting in me taking the heat for things like deadlines without the support to get members of the team to follow. The times I tried to correct this, I took the heat too. I left."

    —White woman, CTO

"Even at the most inclusive workplaces, I've always felt that women were expected to walk a razor-thin line. We had to be ambitious and hardworking, but not too ambitious. We had to speak up for ourselves, but not too much. I've always ended up being viewed as 'difficult' even when I was completely professional (certainly a lot more professional than some of my colleagues)."

    —White woman, data scientist

In the chapters that follow, you'll hear from other members of underrepresented groups who have been subjected, as one of the survey respondents aptly put it, to "death from a thousand paper cuts." Their experiences—echoed by so many others at conferences, in affinity group meetings, in Reddit communities, and in blog posts—show just how deep the problem of inclusion runs in tech workforces.[15] So often diversity is seen as an issue of numbers, of not having enough employees from particular backgrounds and needing to hire more so that next year's DEI report looks better than this year's. But you can't just bring people into a dysfunctional culture and hope it will work out.

I sincerely appreciate the intent of many of the programs that companies deploy to hire more employees from underrepresented groups. However, creating significant change is not easy when you have a culture with a long tradition of advantaging and protecting one group over others. It requires a systemic approach to building environments that are truly supportive of inclusivity and creativity.

The Way Forward

Among the many important programs we developed and deployed at AnitaB.org was the Technical Executive Forum (TEF), a small and invite-only program for technical executives held at the Grace Hopper Celebration. The purpose of TEF was to bring in technical leaders to confidentially discuss their approach to innovation and inclusivity with their peers. These conversations, and the successes of at least some of the TEF participants, showed me that companies that made difficult and significant changes to their cultures were able to achieve meaningful results. They could create cultures where everyone is encouraged to speak up and everyone's ideas are heard and acknowledged. Cultures where everyone's contributions are fairly rewarded. Cultures where all tech workers, no matter their backgrounds, can see people who look like them in leadership positions. Cultures where everyone believes they have a path to success.

To get there, these companies made changes that were systemic in nature. They didn't just make a few tweaks to their hiring practices or appoint someone to be responsible for inclusion efforts (though, done well, these *are* essential tools to build inclusivity). "Increasing diversity" was not just another soundbite recited by their well-meaning CEOs at conferences and in media calls. Instead, these companies were led by CEOs who understood deeply that an inclusive culture must be intertwined with their innovation strategy; they believed deep in their core that to create great new products, you need a diversity of perspectives and ideas. This belief informed every decision they made.

If you are serious about dismantling an unwelcoming, homogeneous environment and increasing the number and participation of technical people from all backgrounds, your organization—led by the CEO and other company executives—must build a culture that values *everyone's* perspectives. The six Cs—creativity, courage, confidence, curiosity, communication, and community—can help you get you there. If you create a culture where everyone speaks up, is curious about others' perspectives, and listens to one another, you will bring talented people—especially from underrepresented groups—out of the shadows to fully participate in the future together.

<**2**>
CREATIVITY

Our business [is] about problem-solving. And that
problem-solving comes down to how many diverse
ideas you have in the mix.

**—Rebecca Parsons, former CTO and CTO Emerita,
Thoughtworks**

Silicon Valley. Even in its infancy, it was the place to be. When I first arrived, it was awash with startups creating silicon architectures for exploring novel chips; eventually their efforts revolutionized computation and gave us much of the technology we have today, including cloud computing and AI. The field was full of promise, excitement, and, most important, innovation. The first startup I worked at was Actel, where I was employee number thirty. The founders, former Intel employees and Stanford engineering graduates who were Egyptian by background, set the tone for the company: creativity was king. Their focus was on mining academic research and experimenting to create a brand-new approach to a programmable architecture. Colleagues and friends, they bonded with each other. And perhaps because they experienced being outsiders in Silicon Valley, they embraced people from many ethnic backgrounds and genders and didn't care where ideas came from as long as they were good.

As a young engineer, I received the message that my contributions were valuable and my voice and opinions mattered. I could bring much of my research results from graduate school to bear on the work I was hired to do. My particular expertise was in the layout and circuit synthesis of devices, focusing on the programmable routing channels. However, I had to work closely with the circuit design and customer software teams to get the best product out. Semiconductor products are inherently more complex than software-only ones. Team members had to collaborate to develop new approaches and practices for all the systems—the hardware, architecture, and software—to work together. The result was a programmable product that changed the way people designed hardware.

This breakthrough was possible because the culture at Actel nurtured creativity. An ethnically and racially diverse staff ensured a healthy diversity of ideas was expressed and shared, and the leadership encouraged cross-disciplinary collaboration and rewarded inventive thinking. Although there were few women, I was treated with respect. I felt like an important team member, included in thoughtful conversations about product features and support. Working on Actel's original product set the stage for my career. There I was recognized for my creativity and contributions, and rewarded with opportunities to take a leadership role in the next-generation architecture, which ultimately led me into leadership positions for future projects. This culture was instrumental in my decision to stay at Actel for eleven years.

· · ·

According to consultancy McKinsey & Company, "Innovation is the ability to conceive, develop, deliver, and scale new products, services, processes, and business models for customers."[1] You know innovation when you see it. *Creativity*—thinking outside the box, solving problems in an original way, and developing ideas efficiently—is its backbone. You cannot be a genuinely forward-looking company if you don't have good ideas to transform into compelling products, services, or processes. That is why creativity is the foundational C in a culture of innovation.

It can be hard to pin down an abstract concept like creativity. But I find writer Maria Popova's definition helpful. She describes it as "a combinatorial force—it thrives on cross-pollinating exist-ing ideas, often across divergent disciplines and sensibilities, and combining them into something new."[2] In a tech organization, creativity is what happens when technical staff contribute their unique ideas to be considered, explored, debated, or combined to create new technologies, products, or ways of doing things.

As Popova explains, having a diversity of perspectives is cru-cial. If everyone brings similar ideas to the table, it's hard to see connections and new possibilities beyond them. It is no wonder that tech workplaces where people from different backgrounds and with different perspectives are able to share their ideas—and see them be appreciated and respected—are fertile ground for cre-ativity and collaboration. These cultures support the intertwined goals of innovation and inclusion by embracing and valuing *every-one's* contributions.

But even in tech companies that catapulted to success with breakthrough inventions, such a culture is rarer than you'd think. As we'll learn later in the chapter, when startups mature and grow, creativity is often stifled. Fostering it in the long term, it turns out, is not easy. It requires attention and intention. But it is possible. The same culture that effortlessly fuels many startups and entrepreneurial ventures can also be nurtured at large tech companies.

In this chapter, we'll go over why creativity is so easily stifled and what makes it ignite, and explore how you can nurture it in your organization. The key, explains Ed Catmull, former president of Pixar and author of *Creativity, Inc.*, is that "the people in the room must view one another as peers; everyone's voice has equal weight."[3] We'll dive deeply into three things you can do to create such spaces and foster a culture of creativity—one that doesn't shut down ideas before they are formed and where all team members are encouraged to contribute, collaborate, and take risks. The three things are:

- **Promote and encourage respect throughout the organization.** Without respect, people are hesitant to express their ideas and contribute to products and processes.

- **Diversify your technical pipeline.** If the best way to boost creativity is by getting ideas from a wider range of sources, then you must ensure your technical pipeline is broadly diverse.

- **Develop the skills of all employees early.** To build a diverse technical pipeline, it's critical that people from all backgrounds are given opportunities early on to develop the skills they need to achieve their potential and contribute at the highest level to your innovation processes.

Once you've started fostering a culture that welcomes creativity, the hard work of creating an environment that *supports* it, as well as collaboration, follows. The rest of the book will show how nurturing courage, confidence, curiosity, communication, and community are, in essence, the heart of that work.

How Creativity Is Smothered—and Ignited

As someone who grew up professionally in Silicon Valley, I know that creativity and innovation are the mantras of entrepreneurs everywhere. And for good reason. Tech startups frequently, almost accidentally, build cultures based on them. Teams come together to solve a particular technological problem. Their survival depends on fresh ideas. With scarce resources, loose hierarchies, and fluid work processes, it's all hands on deck. Employees' contributions, clear and recognized, are influential in the final product. Most founders and their teams experience a deep sense of exploration that leads to new products, as I did at Actel.

But as tech startups mature, they often become victims of their success. On one hand, their growth means they have more access to resources, including staff and money to invest in R&D. But the creative culture that fueled the breakthroughs of their earlier years is damped down as they shift from taking risks and innovating to scaling, creating efficiencies, and seeking stability. Charlan Jeanne Nemeth, professor in the Department of Psychology at the University of California, Berkeley, has found that classic management approaches that organizations tend to adopt as they become more established stifle a culture of creativity. "Most companies, even those considered visionary, emphasize mechanisms of social control rather than innovation. They recognize the power of clear goals, worker participation, consistent feedback, a cohesive workforce, and a reward system that underscores desired behaviors and values," she writes. "In fact, the spark that companies are likely to ignite is not innovation or risk-taking but rather loyalty and commitment."[4]

As tech firms grow, their processes and hierarchies become hardened, limiting the freedom to experiment or bring new ideas to the table. They become more conservative and keep going to the same well—the same approaches—that originally made them successful. And eventually that well dries up.

When I was a graduate student at Caltech, I spent the summer of 1980 at Digital Equipment Corporation (DEC) in Hudson, Massachusetts. At the time, DEC was considered one of the most cutting-edge technology companies, and its computers, the DECSYSTEM-20 and the VAX, were the industry standard. I programmed on those machines for most of my grad student career. And yet by 1998 the company was a shadow of what it once had been, and was acquired by Compaq. DEC made some of the classic business decisions that lead to a decline in innovation: not embracing new architectures quickly enough, holding on too tightly to products that bring in most of the revenue, and underestimating the value of thinking up future products. In the end, the company failed to meet the demands of the shifting market.

This pattern of rapid innovation and success, followed by years of innovation stagnation and failure, is common for technology firms. History is riddled with stories of companies that, like DEC, either disappeared or became significantly less relevant as they lost their creative edge.

I remember the day my friend Anita Borg, who was at a research lab, showed me an early version of the Netscape web browser. My head nearly exploded as I considered the possibilities of what this technology allowed. But as Netscape got bigger and eventually was bought by AOL, it was overshadowed by other browsers that dominated the market by evolving more quickly.[5] More recently, other companies have fallen because their creativity was stifled by the hardening of work processes and leadership hierarchies: Kodak, Xerox, Nokia, Research in Motion, and Hewlett-Packard, to name a few. You may think these examples are historical and don't represent the status quo of today. But DEC was around for longer than Google has been as of this writing, and for about as long as Amazon has existed. Creating a culture of creativity is not easy, but it is critical for survival.

Tech companies face another hindrance here, too: the myth of the lone genius. As a society, we are fascinated by the exceptionally creative. From Benjamin Franklin to Nikola Tesla to Jeff Bezos, our desire to worship them has birthed the narrative that most inventions are the product of a brilliant (and often eccentric) mind working in isolation.[6] This couldn't be further from the truth. Given the number of books on the collaborative nature of innovation, it's fair to say that, at least academically, the concept is well established—and is also professed by many tech leaders. But within companies, the myth that creativity is limited to a chosen few persists.

Perhaps the media has something to do with it. Consider the coverage of technology superstars such as Mark Zuckerberg, whose claim to have come up with Facebook entirely on his own has been contested (even in legal court), or Steve Jobs, whose business brilliance often eclipsed the work of the many people who built Apple's most profitable products. After all, you don't typically see a photo of the whole department responsible for a technological feat on the cover of *Fortune, Fast Company,* or *Forbes.* You're more likely to see a picture of the CEO, the CTO, or whoever is considered the principal innovator.

Internally, the cultures of many tech startups is built on an obsession we explored in chapter 1: that of the lone genius archetype. At its heart, the archetype embodies the beliefs that creativity and talent are innate, invention is the result of individual effort, needing help or working collaboratively is a sign of weakness or lack of brilliance, and a single point of view—not a diversity of ideas—drives companies forward.

These beliefs, of course, are the opposite of the attitude organizations need to produce meaningful, sustained innovation. In his book *The Diversity Bonus*, Scott E. Page, a professor of complex systems, political science, and economics at the University of Michigan, explains that to solve tough problems, creating a team with cognitive diversity—which includes identity diversity—can produce positive outcomes. Bob Nunn, former CEO of smart sensor manufacturer Everactive, is a strong believer in drawing on a variety of backgrounds, viewpoints, and skill sets. "When you start bringing people that came from a poor upbringing where they had to fight and scrap all the way, and others who had a silver spoon [growing up], it's really an interesting dynamic," he told me. The fact is that creativity thrives when there are many *different* perspectives. "Minority viewpoints have importance and power not just for the value of the ideas themselves," UC Berkeley's Nemeth explains, "but their ability to stimulate creative thought."[7]

One piece of evidence that points to the value of diversity in innovation is the National Center for Women and Information Technology's 2022 report about women's participation in US patents. In the forty-one years covered by the study (1980 to 2020), mixed-gender teams produced the most highly cited patents, with citation rates 30 percent to 50 percent higher than the norm.[8]

As Page notes, when people with varying perspectives or ways of thinking collaborate, conflict inevitably follows. But that very conflict is what often leads to breakthrough solutions. Unfortunately, though, people are not wired to pursue healthy conflict or disagreement. In fact, Nemeth explains, "while most of us would like to believe that we are tolerant of dissenting views, the initial inclination of anyone—whether they are management or workers—is to underestimate and resist viewpoints that differ from their own."

Promote and Encourage Respect
Throughout the Organization

To promote a culture of creativity, one where multiple perspectives can be considered and debated, you must start with fostering a diverse workforce that feels comfortable sharing their best ideas freely. It's tempting to assume that this can be accomplished simply by hiring more members of marginalized groups. Over the years, many tech companies I have worked with have focused their DEI programs on hiring with this approach in mind. And make no mistake—bringing a broad range of talent into your organization is absolutely necessary for creativity and innovation to thrive. Without a diversity of perspectives and expertise, you miss out on key ideas and skills that make creative collaboration possible.

But hiring more employees from underrepresented groups is not enough.

Françoise Brougher, former chief operating officer of Pinterest, explains it well. "Companies are very, very, very eager to hire [diverse candidates]," she told me. "But then when you arrive at the company, there is nothing done to enable you to be successful. You [hit] the same barrier because you are a minority. . . . Whatever you say, whatever you do, it's put under this microscope of being a diversity [hire]. So you have much less latitude to be who you are because everything you say and do is overanalyzed by your white men or Indian men colleagues."

While it may help you reach your diversity goals in terms of numbers, hiring people from underrepresented groups won't, by itself, increase creativity in your team or lead to a culture that supports innovation and inclusivity. You must also ensure everyone in the organization is—and feels—respected by both management and their peers.

Respect is the salve that allows constructive conflict to lead to breakthroughs, rather than the kinds of barriers Françoise and other people from underrepresented groups end up hitting over and over. When people treat each other with respect, they are more open to new viewpoints. They are more willing to listen to and engage with colleagues who have different perspectives, backgrounds, skill sets, and expertise. But just as important, when the exchange of radically different viewpoints leads to conflict, which according to Page is inevitable, respect for one another helps everyone get past the discomfort that a candid debate is likely to produce.

As Gary Pisano, Harvard Business School professor and author of *Creative Construction: The DNA of Sustained Innovation*, points out, "unvarnished candor is critical to innovation because it is the means by which ideas evolve and improve."[9] But, he cautions, candor can also be uncomfortable, especially in organizations where "to challenge too strongly is to risk looking like you are not a team player." Given how common it is for behaviors to be perceived through biased, gendered, and racialized lenses—for example, women are "too nice," Black men are "angry" or "aggressive," Latinas are "feisty"—being radically candid presents significant risks to members of underrepresented groups in most organizations. At the same time, "unvarnished candor" for the sake of "creative conflict" is often used as cover for overt bias and aggression. Someone might attack a colleague's personality rather than critique their ideas, and then call their peer "thin-skinned" or fault them for "not being able to take criticism well" when they call it out. Both of these situations lead employees of underrepresented groups to hold back, diminishing their potential to deliver novel innovations.

But in environments where people show respect for other people's skills, perspectives, and experiences, everyone—regardless of gender, race, physical ability, or any other aspect of identity—is more willing to contribute and engage in candid discussions without fear of being penalized. "Providing and accepting frank criticism is one of the hallmarks of respect," Pisano writes.[10]

Respect, in short, makes the difficult, often uncomfortable, and messy process of creativity go smoother. It helps tech organizations become the kind of place where, in Catmull's words, "people want to hear each other's [ideas], even when those [ideas] are challenging."[11]

Respect also creates environments where people feel trusted to bring their most creative ideas, and to do their best. That's the kind of culture Lisa Su, the CEO of AMD, and Mark Papermaster, its CTO and executive vice president, fostered when they were tasked with turning the chip maker around. Founded in 1969, Advanced Micro Devices cut its teeth in the computer chip space as a second source supplier to Intel. After the two companies parted ways, AMD started producing its own chips (reverse-engineering Intel's), and soon became competitive in the semiconductor field. But for decades, its chips were plagued by performance problems. By 2013 the company had fallen significantly behind its competitors and was on the brink of bankruptcy.[12]

At the top of Su and Papermaster's turnaround plan was creating great products. They drew on her leadership style to set the tone for the company's innovation goals. "As a leader, I enjoy inspiring teams to come together and accomplish what might have seemed impossible," Su shared with me. "[This] requires creating an environment that includes a talented team, compelling vision, clarity in purpose, and a sense of urgency to achieve our shared goals." And they also leaned on Papermaster's vision to create a culture of quality products and execution. "Culture is foundational. But if you don't have a competitive product, it doesn't do any good to have a great engineering and collaborative culture," he told me. "We had to create a culture of execution, where we delivered what we said we were going to do, when we said we would do it, and with the right quality."

They set their engineers to build a new high-performance computing architecture to compete with giants like Intel and Nvidia. They knew that, to accomplish this innovation feat, the company's leadership needed to prioritize creativity. So they put collaboration front and center. "One of the ways we did so," explained Papermaster, "was by tapping bright, ambitious, and broadly diverse people to drive creativity at AMD." To support their culture efforts, they leaned on a long-held value at the company. "AMD had a storied history of respecting its people," he said. "This led to a culture where employees knew they were trusted and valued."

It worked.

AMD released the new chip architecture, Zen, which was 50 percent faster than its previous one, in 2017.[13] In 2023 it finally overtook Intel as the market leader in computer processors.

Respected, trusted, valued. If your entire workforce doesn't feel these, then it doesn't matter how many members of underrepresented groups you bring into your organization. They won't contribute their unique perspectives to help create your next big product or idea—and they won't stick around for long. Nurturing a culture of creativity anchored in respect allows *all* employees to share their brilliance and develop the breakthrough innovations your organization depends on for its survival.

Diversify Your Technical Pipeline

If every voice is to have equal weight for creativity to thrive, as Catmull suggests, then to foster that kind of culture you must ensure every person is given an opportunity to grow, develop, and shine. A tech organization is only as good as the people who build its future. And yet, many of the most talented people in yours are likely flying under the radar.

The technical pipeline is one of the most important assets, if not *the* most important, of a tech organization. It's an investment in the future. Companies know this, so they nurture that pipeline of talented technologists and feed it carefully. Many offer a career ladder that rewards employees who choose to stay on the technical side rather than move to a management role.

In many organizations, the top of this technical ladder is the "fellow" designation. Its gendered name bothers me, but that doesn't change the fact that staff in technical roles aspire to achieve it. A fellow typically has the most senior role on the technical ladder and is equivalent to a vice president. Organizations develop their fellows programs to ensure that they have depth in the staff who are developing key technical ideas. Although not every company has a fellows track, the availability of both a technical and a management ladder is typical.

For organizations whose future relies on technical product portfolios, ensuring the technical ladder supports the kind of genuine collaboration that only comes from diversity is critical. Unfortunately, most fellows programs lack the very diversity that creative cultures so desperately need. The underrepresentation of certain groups is often rooted in a long history of missed opportunities and decades of institutional bias that can take years to dismantle. But it *can* be done.

Diane Bryant, former group president at Intel, was instrumental in diversifying and transforming the fellow track at the company. In her earlier years, the program was led by a white man who was openly biased against women. "He was my direct manager at a point in time, and he was open about his views on women working. He said that a woman's job is to care for the home and family, and that I didn't deserve to hold my job because I was taking a job from a man who deserved it," she shared with me. "He ran the fellows program for years and—not coincidently—Intel had no women fellows. You had a white man running the process and a voting panel of male fellows deciding who would be promoted. The committee was all men because there weren't any women fellows to participate. It was a self-fulfilling prophecy that more men—and no women—would be promoted."

In 2006, two years after she became a vice president, Bryant took over as leader of the program at the request of Paul Otellini, Intel's CEO at the time. Otellini recognized the flawed design of the existing structure and wanted to fix it. Bryant made two significant changes. First, she included senior women vice presidents on the panel—the only way to expand it to include women. The men were enraged. They complained that Bryant was changing the long-standing rule that only fellows could be judges. Second, Bryant instituted a five-year tenure for service on the panel. She told several male fellows who had been on the panel for a long time that they could no longer serve as judges. "I received very hostile and confrontational feedback, like 'I've been on that panel for ten years. How dare you kick me off?'" Bryant said. But she pushed through her changes with the support of Otellini. Four years later—and more than two decades after she joined the company in the engineering department—Intel announced its first female fellow.

"By 2015 we had six women fellows, including two senior fellows, the highest position an individual contributor can hold. There were roughly thirty total fellows then, so twenty percent of them were women, compared to the historical zero percent," Bryant shared. "Breaking the vicious cycle and creating an equitable and unbiased system was as simple as balancing the makeup of the people in decision-making roles."

Bryant had to systematically dismantle an entire fellow selection process that was at one point overtly discriminatory and had bias baked right into it. But it's equally important to change smaller processes that leave the door open just enough for bias to sneak in, like deciding which qualifications are required for consideration as a fellow. All too often these kinds of criteria are opaque and unclear, and the feedback provided can be equally vague. Many companies do this deliberately. Deep technical expertise can look radically different depending on the technology or discipline, so the same criteria might not readily apply to experts in different areas. Also, selection committees like to base their decisions on how much a candidate's contributions impacted products with serious revenue potential.

But without a transparent process and selection criteria, it's difficult for candidates to know what they are aiming for—or even if aiming would make a difference at all. In 2005 researchers at Yale University found that "people making hiring decisions construct criteria of merit congenial to the particular strengths of members of the advantaged or dominant group." In other words, they move the goalposts. The researchers also found that when decision-makers establish clear criteria before reviewing candidates' credentials, discrimination is all but eliminated.[14] Although selecting a fellow is not the same as hiring a job candidate, it's not hard to imagine that similar mechanisms might be at play in both situations when standard criteria are absent.

Opaqueness has an unexpected impact on many young and ambitious engineers who are passionate about technology but also desire significant leadership roles. As technical fellows, they would have the opportunity to lead technical innovations, a starkly different path than those who choose to be managers where their impact is in leading teams. But these engineers see more examples of successful leaders who chose the management path, and the trade-offs of doing so versus following a technical path are not always explained effectively. Unless they have a sponsor, who believes in them and can help them understand how they could qualify for a promotion to a technical leadership role, they may choose to pursue a management role.

Develop the Skills of All Employees Early

When developing a diverse pipeline for the technical track, it's essential to create targeted programs, start early, and think long-term. That's what Bridget Frey, the CTO at digital real estate firm Redfin, has done.

Frey is committed to developing a diverse group of senior technical talent. At Redfin, "a tech lead is one of our most senior individual contributor roles," she explained. "It's not a management role, but it's a leadership role within tech." The challenge is that tech leads, as they are in many companies, are "the least diverse pocket of our talent. . . . They are largely white and Asian and largely male." So, the company started a tech lead development program to address this issue.

"We have a diverse group of people early in their career, but it will take time for them to get there," Frey said. "We started a program where we essentially apprentice folks who are senior engineers. . . . They are mentored by someone who helps them develop their careers. They can shadow work that someone is doing that's more advanced than what they're currently doing." As Frey told me, the goal of the program is "finding the spaces that feel closed and opening them up."

This apprenticeship model provides technologists opportunities to develop a deeper understanding of what it looks like to be in a creative role and allows them to move into a tech lead position more quickly. Especially since the fellow and tech lead paths are not always clearly defined, creating apprenticeships that pair talented, high-potential employees from underrepresented groups with successful fellows can have a lasting impact on their careers and your organization.

Like Redfin, AMD focuses on identifying talent from underrepresented groups as early as possible. According to Mark Papermaster, the company has "a very strict bar to achieve this level of fellow. But we started creating early identification, a pipeline for women and minorities so that they could pass that bar."

Kevin Scott, CTO of Microsoft, explained that twice a year his company's leadership looks at all staff members who are candidates to be promoted to distinguished and fellow roles. One of several considerations in the process is how diverse those populations are. If there are no candidates for promotion, they look throughout the company for high potentials and provide them with challenging assignments to prove themselves.

Over the years, Scott has noticed that team members often follow a management career path rather than an individual contributor (IC) track. "They will do that . . . because they either don't realize they can get promoted, recognized, and rewarded on the IC track, or they think that's too hard to do," he said. "I've found it important to find those high-potential people and convince them that they want to follow the IC track."

Like Frey, Scott, and Papermaster, Mike Schroepfer, former CTO at Meta, formerly Facebook, believes in investing in a diversity of talent by identifying and developing high potentials as early as possible. "We assess our talent and invest in their future, which is also investing in *our* future," he told me. At Facebook, that meant reviewing the skills that promising, broadly diverse staff were missing. "For example, they haven't led a cross-functional project yet, gone deep in this technical area, or [do not have] enough exposure to this part of the management team," he said. "The output of our review was a plan of how to expose people to these [skills], to give them the opportunities so that when a role opens, you have someone who you've been developing for a while . . . . [and you can] say, well, this person's ready to go and is ready to move into the role." This approach is based on principles that Mike continues to believe in and practice in his work today.

Ana Pinczuk, a former tech executive at Anaplan, leveraged a unique approach to developing talent that she calls the three Es. "When I think about building talent," she shared with me, "I think about *exposure*: Do they get exposure to the right people and opportunities? I look at *experience*: Are they getting the projects they should? Are they getting the skills and experience? And then there is the *educational* element: Are we giving them the tools that they need?"

A culture of creativity depends on having access to as many ideas and perspectives as possible. A robust and diverse technical pipeline is your best bet to get there. Make sure *everyone* in your organization has access to it. Shine a light on the technical career path and what it means to be successful in it. And help every single employee develop the skills they need to share their best ideas so, together, you can develop great innovations.

Let Your Mission Guide Creativity

Diane Greene is a Silicon Valley legend. She is one of the cofounders of VMware and was its CEO for over ten years. Subsequently, she served on Google's board and led its cloud division for four years. Before VMware, she'd been involved in two startups, and those experiences led her to be very thoughtful about the culture she promoted during its early years.

"When we finally started VMware, I wanted all the founders to cowrite and sign a mission and vision statement. It proved really valuable, to have a conscious set of principles you care about as we developed the product and created the virtualization market; both were quite complex," she explained. "The founders . . . were engineers. And that built tremendous trust among the engineering ranks because if there was a decision that people didn't understand, they would go to the founders." After she left VMware, Greene heard many people tell her how unusually collaborative it was. That collaborative style, guided by a clear mission and vision, was fundamental to the company's success at the time.

A clear mission is key to fostering a creative culture that fuels innovation and inclusion. If your team understands your company's larger purpose, they can channel their efforts toward fulfilling it. As they collaborate and develop original solutions to complex problems, their work will align with the mission.

That was Darby Dunn's goal when she set out to build the culture of Commonwealth Fusion Systems (CFS), where she is vice president of production. As CFS's third hire, she had a lot of time to talk with the founders about the kind of culture they wanted. She also worked hard to ensure those she hired aligned with the culture's principles. "We were very careful about the folks hired, especially right off the bat," she told me. "At a very small company, the first ten people you hire set the culture of the company, and then the ten people that each of them hires get us to one hundred people. And that first group determines the company culture."

One of the first questions she and her team ask applicants is, "Why CFS?" "We look for people who want to learn and are looking to absorb new information. To me that means that you're not comfortable with the status quo," she explained. "We want people who can innovate, improve, and learn more about the scientific aspect of ideas and suggestions. We are trying to solve and build some complex stuff. So, are you able to take what comes your way and decide if you need to pivot?"

A clear and compelling mission can inspire and motivate teams to apply creativity to complex problems. Mary Lou Jepsen is most famous as cofounder and the first CTO of One Laptop per Child and, more recently, cofounder of Openwater. Previously, she held positions at Facebook and Google, and she has over two hundred patents. Jepsen has a long history of leading creative tech organizations. "[At Openwater] we have a mission-based organization.... The way you actually impact humanity seems to be through companies because you develop products that can help lives, [however] that is," she told me. "With that as a focus, that motivates the entire team."

Through my leadership at AnitaB.org, I've found nothing is more powerful than having an entire team believe their work could impact the world. Regularly articulating the ways in which your product affects people, and highlighting how your staff's ideas and collaborative efforts directly contribute to the organization's mission, helps to fuel a culture of creativity and innovation. Jepsen, who is both creative and inclusive, found a similar outcome with her current role.

Most companies espouse the need to be creative. Unfortunately, like commitments to diversity and inclusion, it has become another sound bite, words with no substance. I encourage you to consider what creativity means to you and your organization and to demonstrate to your employees how they can be part of the future. Creativity and collaboration are the foundations of innovation.

ACTIONS

To create a culture of creativity, seek out diverse points of view and perspectives and help your employees see how their ideas contribute to your mission.

Promote and Encourage Respect Throughout the Organization

Model creative conflict discussion within your team. Demonstrate with your behavior how ideas are listened to, challenged, and carried forward. Regularly review your product development thought process and the evolution of ideas. Regularly consider how the decisions of your group impact other organizations.

Manage challenging conflict. Communicate that negative, aggressive, and disrespectful behavior is not tolerated; emphasize respect instead. Model interventions in real time, calling out microaggressions and aggressive behavior. Educate your team about helpful ally behaviors.

Diversify Your Technical Pipeline

Communicate the requirements for promotion to the top of the technical track. Review, articulate, and publish the criteria required to be promoted to technical fellow levels in an accessible way. Offer training that develops employees' skills in areas that are important. If your company is not promoting many people, consider other ideas for development, like global assignments, role rotations, and other innovative roles.

Include members of underrepresented groups in promotion committees. Ensure that the committee responsible for promotion decisions is not solely composed of people from the majority population, especially in the technical fellow pipeline. If promotion decisions are made by a few people, find ways to provide them with diverse perspectives, including technical, geographic, age, sexual orientation, racial, ethnic, and gender diversity.

Develop the Skills of All Employees Early

Regularly meet with leadership to identify gaps in your technical pipeline. If your pipeline is not diverse, actively seek out high-potential individuals for further development. Create opportunities for your staff, technical leads, and leaders across the organization to meet in group discussions or technical presentations. Unless your people are exposed to situations where they can demonstrate their talents and skills, they won't be noticed.

Develop an apprenticeship program for high-potential technical talent. Pair up employees who show promise with technical leads and fellows. Make sure there is a broadly diverse set of participants, considering gender, ethnic, racial, sexual orientation, age, and technical diversity. If your workforce is global, be sure to include talent from each geographic region.

Provide educational and skill development in key technical areas. Tech talks, job rotations, and free time to dedicate to one's personal projects are great ways for people to experience cross-learning and broaden their knowledge and skills.

Let Your Mission Guide Creativity

Clearly communicate your company's vision to motivate creativity. Discuss the importance of the mission with job candidates and new employees. Regularly talk about the impact your products have on the market and world.

Provide a clear articulation of success. Articulate the problems that need to be solved to accomplish the mission. Frequently remind your team what success looks like. Regularly emphasize the opportunities and excitement in doing something that has never been done.

‹ 3 ›
COURAGE

We speak truth to power. You have to have the courage
to do that. And you have to create an environment
where people are willing to do that and not be afraid.
—Thuan Pham, former CTO, Uber and Coupang

The courage to take risks is at the heart of my story.

After eleven years at Actel, where I had worked my way up to director of software, I joined an early-stage startup called Malleable Technologies as a member of the founding management team. I was the fourth employee and the vice president of engineering. When I started, we had funding for six months and an idea for programmable architecture. It was a wild ride. We secured more funding, grew the company to fifty people, and developed a chip design, the digital-signal-processing coding to turn the programmable processor into a voice over IP product, and the design software that customers needed to use our product. We eventually sold the company to PMC-Sierra for a significant profit. Most would call the entire process a success.

Startups are inherently risk-taking endeavors. To face the uncertainties of launching something new, their founders need courage—the fortitude to put an idea forward or tackle a challenge despite the fear of failure. But startups and companies succeed in the long term when that mindset trickles down to everyone in the organization.

A culture of courage—where contributions are welcomed from anyone, and every team member is encouraged to take risks while being treated with respect by their teammates—was critical to Malleable's early success. The chip design, software, and product engineering teams faced many technical hurdles. Ensuring that everyone in these teams was respectful while learning from each other was imperative. The founder was responsible for the novel chip architecture. Our chip design team was internally led by a highly competent circuit designer who worked with an experienced chip architect—who was a woman. Our engineering team included knowledgeable chip designers, an outstanding woman who managed the chip verification and validation process, a compiler expert, and an extraordinary logic synthesis expert. Finally, we had a set of digital signal processing engineers with deep expertise in voice-over IP coding.

During the eighteen-month development cycle of our product, we worked together, listened to each other, and encouraged every staff member to participate. Engineers with wildly different focuses shared their knowledge across functions. Individuals dared to surface ideas outside their area of expertise if they thought they could help another team. We didn't have the luxury of making decisions in isolation—and we couldn't afford to exclude ideas based solely on who was giving them. Every idea needed to be voiced and heard, or we risked missing out on an opportunity. It required courage from everyone.

However, in the early days I was naive about risk-taking cultures and the courage that naturally accompanies them. As organizations grow and become more complex, courage must be nurtured actively, or it dissipates quickly. After a couple of years at Malleable, I watched the culture that had fueled our successes go sour. Late in the product development cycle, when problems occurred—as they always do for complex products—frustrations were high and staff members began lashing out instead of listening to and respecting each other's ideas.

One day, a senior engineer whom I will call Otto belittled me at an all-engineering meeting, questioning my view of the algorithms we were developing. Back then it was unusual (and still is today) to find a woman at the head of an engineering department, and some engineers had no problem expressing their blatant sexist feelings about it. Otto was one of them. Instead of debating ideas on their merit, he was disrespectful and mean-spirited in front of the entire staff, determined to display his own prowess, a common habit among individual members of engineering teams.

Although I made sure he was held accountable for his behavior privately, I didn't do so publicly. At that moment, I let it slide. I yearned to be recognized for my technical contribution, even as I was painfully aware of the negative attention that came my way in every technical role I accepted. I didn't want to be seen as riled up by Otto in public. In hindsight, by allowing his behavior to go unchecked publicly, I unwittingly damaged the culture of courage that had benefited our company so much. Otto had good ideas about our overall product. But his lack of respect and open contempt when expressing dissent dampened everyone's enthusiasm for voicing *their* ideas. Few want to be shamed and badgered as I had been. As a leader, I wasn't just responsible for developing this product; I was also responsible for organizational challenges. It was my job to set the tone for the entire engineering staff, to create a culture where everyone felt safe enough to rise to the occasion, to share their perspective, and to know that they would be listened to with genuine curiosity.

I learned then that a culture of courage invites precisely the kind of productive conflict and risk-taking that technical innovation requires. Disrespect and bias shut it down. To create a culture of courage requires:

- Creating opportunities for all employees to contribute

- Assigning high-risk, high-reward assignments broadly

- Supporting employees who speak truth to power

The goal of creating this kind of culture is to ensure everyone in the organization feels supported enough to contribute their very best—and that the best ideas have a chance to be surfaced and inform your forward-looking projects. When a tech organization is staffed by people who feel safe enough to stand up for their perspectives, both innovation and inclusivity thrive.

Why a Culture of Courage Matters

Courage is vital in technical organizations. Exploring what is possible and what is helpful to your customers is unapologetically exciting. But developing a new technology is also an exercise in taking risks. New products either break fresh technical ground or get replaced by others that do. Coming up with novel and untested ventures carries the risk of failure—of wasted resources and damaged reputations. It takes courage to try new approaches and push forward in the face of uncertainty when the stakes are high.

If you are a technical leader, you need your people to summon the courage to offer the best that they've got. You need them to bring every plausible, helpful suggestion to the table to be vetted. You need them to question how things are done. You need them to experiment with new ways of doing things. You need them to be open to listening to others and giving other people chances, even if doing so might be risky.

But all these essential actions are what people tend to be most averse to. "It's natural for people to hold back ideas, be reluctant to ask questions, and shy away from disagreeing with the boss," explains Amy Edmondson, professor of leadership at Harvard Business School. "Given this tendency, the free exchange of ideas, concerns, and questions is routinely hindered—far more than most managers realize."[1] In other words, the things that we need our technical people to do the most are things most of us are naturally inclined *not* to do.

It is particularly hard for those who are the "only one" in the room to make suggestions, ask questions, or express concerns. Although courage is in no short supply among tech employees from marginalized groups, raising new thoughts or calling out the status quo is intimidating and, frankly, not always appreciated, as the microaggressions and blatant bias that often follow make clear. Feeling dismissed, talked over, or excluded takes a toll and can dampen their willingness to put themselves out there. The price they pay for doing so can be high.

Melissa Williams at Emory University and Larissa Tiedens at Stanford University conducted a meta-analysis of seventy-one studies examining the backlash women experience from colleagues when engaging in behaviors otherwise associated positively with men. They found that "compared to men, women were much more likely to be punished for showing dominant behaviors. That is, assertive behaviors like asking for a raise or talking during a meeting can carry a substantial professional risk for women."[2]

When you promote courage in your culture, you empower *everyone* in the organization to take risks, speak up, and listen—no matter their background or expertise. When I worked at Actel and other semiconductor companies, many engineers had a deep knowledge of circuit design. But they distrusted software engineers, who, in turn, didn't respect the circuit designers. The product development process often suffered as a result of their siloed behavior. The hardware designers, for example, would implement a solution in the hardware that would be much better implemented in the software. The most successful engineering leaders find ways to encourage the best solutions from *everyone*.

Engineering leaders also signal that they value people's putting themselves out there by treating these acts of courage with the respect they deserve: by listening, acknowledging, and rewarding them, especially when the risk of failure is great. When a tech culture does not nurture courage, many of the best ideas are often whispered among colleagues at the end of a meeting and don't have a chance to be considered. Or a team works around a badly broken system that remains in place while many who know it doesn't work lack the courage to question the approach. You develop a world-class, innovative organization by creating an environment where everyone feels safe to speak up, to be candid and vulnerable—to summon the courage to take a risk.

Helping every member of your organization understand that an essential aspect of their job is to take risks is more challenging than it looks. Creating a safe environment where people don't fear being rejected or dismissed for their contributions requires a concerted effort. The payoff, however, is not just a healthier culture. It's a more innovative one.

Create Opportunities for All Employees to Contribute

As an engineering leader, I've often become hyperfocused on the technical challenge in front of me. It takes effort to step back from analytical problem-solving and notice who is participating in discussions and brainstorming and, more importantly, who is not.

Developing a culture of courage starts with paying close attention to every team member and recognizing when they need support to feel safe enough to take a risk. Like many engineers, Kevin Scott, CTO at Microsoft, doesn't naturally feel comfortable speaking up. "I'm an introvert by nature. In the past, I found it very difficult to break into the conversation," he told me. "I would sit in meetings and have something important that I wanted to say, that I think would be valuable to the conversation, and not say anything just because it was uncomfortable to break into that conversation." He admits that as he became more senior, he forgot how hard it is to speak up. "Today, as soon as I physically demonstrate my desire to speak, just because I'm the CTO people are already paying attention to me. They will pause the conversation to let me break in," he explained.

At first, Scott didn't notice the people sitting in meetings with him who were never speaking. He would assume that they didn't have anything to say. Eventually, he realized that they were having difficulty speaking up for reasons that had nothing to do with their competence or ability. "This tiny realization that this was happening in my own meetings was very helpful," he said. "I started calling on people. For example, 'I know this person is brilliant, and they haven't said anything—so I'm going to call on them.'" Being aware that some staff might need more support is crucial.

Sameer Halepete, vice president of VLSI Engineering at Nvidia, told me he systematically pays attention to who is speaking and who might be holding back in meetings. During creative discussions, Halepete works hard to identify team members who are hesitant to add something. "I scan the room and see who wants to speak, who is looking to contribute but cannot cross that threshold to speak up," he told me. "But by pausing the meeting and asking for their feedback, ideas surface that are new and innovative."

Although calling on people to encourage them to participate, as Scott and Halepete do, is often effective, be aware some people are more comfortable providing suggestions in smaller settings. As Susan Cain articulates so well in *Quiet,* a book about the power of introversion, some employees prefer to offer their views if you ask them after the meeting.[3] Leaders must find the delicate balance between ensuring employees are heard and following their communication preferences.

For some people, actively promoting courage may seem counter to a culture of success. Shouldn't a successful organization advocate hiring people who are willing to put themselves out there in the first place? If they don't have the courage to speak up, maybe they haven't earned the right to be heard. Replace them with people who do! I'm sure engineers like Otto would feel that way.

But leaders like Scott and Halepete understand that honoring every person's perspective is the best path to sustainable innovation. They also understand that those who feel like *the only one* may be less likely to offer their ideas. Bob Nunn, former CEO of Everactive, told me how he encourages all team members to have the courage to share their ideas. "Sometimes not everyone with a good idea speaks up, especially if they are one of a few," he explained. "So then I go back to the [company's] value statements and [tell them], 'Part of the reason that you're here is we want that opinion that no one else has on the table, to challenge everybody.'" Reminding these team members that their perspective matters, that it is important for the success of the company, and that you will listen to them, is the nudge many employees need to summon the courage to bring forth their boldest ideas.

Of course, a CEO has influence to nurture a culture where everyone feels empowered. But leaders at all levels can do the same. Over the years, I've experimented with many approaches so that every person has a chance to present their perspective. But equally important is ensuring that other leaders offer that chance too. It's critical that when reluctant risk-takers finally speak, everyone listens. In her work, Edmondson explores the need to train both individuals and the team in how to engage in *candid sharing of ideas and concerns.* Each of us must have the courage to speak up, but the entire team needs to develop listening skills and provide thoughtful feedback for a culture of courage to thrive.

Finally, Edmondson advocates for *normalizing vulnerability* to create psychologically safe organizations where everyone feels they can contribute, which can also advance a culture of courage.[4] Sharing their ideas is scary for many people because they feel exposed and vulnerable. That's why showing vulnerability is an act of courage in and of itself. You can encourage people to feel more comfortable with vulnerability by demonstrating it. If you aren't sure about a suggestion, be open about it, sharing the factors that you are considering. And more importantly, be open about outcomes, even if an idea didn't pan out.

When I was at Malleable, we discussed the choices we made about a vendor or design tools, which for a startup were extraordinarily expensive, and debated decisions before they were made—and after. We debated, for example, the product definitions and whether we should allow customer processor programming and customization. Talking about ideas and decisions that failed—and showing what you've learned—encourages others to offer risky perspectives even if there's no guarantee they will work. You can and should applaud the person who chose to share.

One final note about courage and risk-taking—terms that I often use interchangeably. As your employees embrace courage, and as you encourage it, taking risks will often be how that manifests. The risk may be speaking up, accepting a stretch assignment, or experimenting with a novel solution. For me, courage expresses that moment when I am terrified and I move forward nonetheless. Similarly, risk-taking happens when I embrace discomfort and move to accept a tough assignment. Courage is deep inside us, waiting to show itself. While you're building the culture you want, provide opportunities for all your people to look within to find their own courage. Remember, risk-taking is about encouraging people to accept or suggest opportunities where you don't know the outcome. That's why one of the most important aspects of a culture of courage is embracing failure. Failure is one of our greatest teachers, and the way in which you, as the leader, acknowledge shortcomings while still celebrating your staff's decisions to take risks will determine the culture you'll have.

Assign High-Risk, High-Reward Assignments Broadly

Many companies create their futures through task forces and high-risk projects whose plans challenge their current products. Involvement in these efforts is coveted for a good reason: many successful technical leaders can trace the moment their careers took off to these opportunities. High-risk, high-reward assignments are highly effective at allowing employees to exercise their courage muscles, step up, and even get comfortable with the risk of failure of a venture.

At Actel, I benefited greatly from being offered a risky but high-profile assignment. I was asked (after putting my name in the hat) to lead the development of a brand-new release of customer software called Isis. Actel, a chip company, desperately needed to ramp up its expertise in software development, as the current offering it provided customers with was rudimentary at best.

However, the company didn't have many people with the required expertise. Leading this cross-functional effort involved encouraging critical figures from marketing, sales, chip design, software engineering, and user interface to collaborate to develop new approaches. The new design software was wildly successful with our customers when it was finally released. My role as leader of this project gave me excellent visibility within the company. As a technologist, it also allowed me to learn more about the roles around the organization, including marketing and sales. Cross-functional opportunities are widely viewed as a way for high-potential individuals to grow. Shortly after the product's success, I was promoted to engineering director, my first significant promotion.

The importance of this assignment to my career was not lost on me. Unfortunately, this kind of opportunity isn't often given to people who are an only. An article by Erin Macke, Gabriela Gall Rosa, Shannon Gilmartin, and Caroline Simard in the *MIT Sloan Management Review* reports there is a significant gender gap in the leadership of high-profile projects. "Scholars have long identified a gender gap in access to assignments—large in scope, highly visible, and strategically important—that are essential to career advancement," the researchers say. "An estimated 70 percent of leadership development occurs through experiential learning, especially the kind offered by these challenging stretch assignments. Yet women are largely overlooked for challenging work assignments."[5]

In an article in *Harvard Business Review*, Joan C. Williams and Marina Multhaup explain that women and people of color are less likely than white men to be assigned what they call "glamour work," an assignment that "gets you noticed by higher-ups, gives you the opportunity to stretch your skills with a new challenge, and can lead to your next promotion." In a study Williams and Multhaup conducted of engineers, they found that "female engineers of color were 35 percent less likely than white men to report having equal access to desirable assignments; white women were 20 percent less likely."[6] Instead, they're often handed the office housework—taking notes in meetings, planning social events, ordering lunch, and so on—that doesn't contribute to actual results.[7]

One of the most critical decisions technical leaders make is the assignment of projects. Many executives take a low-risk (and low-reward) approach when they choose whom to lead high-risk efforts, assigning essential tasks to the most "familiar" employees, those they trust and like. Because of managers' implicit assumptions of what talent ought to look like, these employees often look like them—meaning mostly male and mostly white and Asian. Yet assigning glamorous or high-risk, high-reward assignments equitably is critical for creating a culture of courage because it signals to all employees that risk-taking by *everyone* in the organization is welcomed.

I met Mike Schroepfer, the CTO of Meta for many years, at AnitaB.org's Technical Executive Forum, a meeting for engi-

FROM THE SURVEY

"I remember as a young female engineer being the only one asked to take meeting notes. As I advanced in my career, I have made sure to rotate this task around [my] team."

—Asian woman, consultant

"Getting my hands slapped for taking risks has made me pull back, due to financial obligations."

—White woman, data scientist

neering executives to learn from one another. A white man, Schroepfer is passionate about creating a culture of courage and is particularly conscious of the obstacles technical people from marginalized groups face when taking risks. He made sure to assign high-risk, high-reward assignments equitably among his team members. But he cautions that developing courage through these stretch assignments requires a long-term investment. "It's sort of five years of prep work you need to do to make sure that at every turn you're challenging people with different backgrounds to develop their skills and their reputation," he explained. "When the opportunity opens up, they're the obvious choice because they're best qualified for the open position."

Nick Donofrio, the former CTO of IBM, was well-known for ensuring that staff from many underrepresented groups were considered for important assignments. He understood these high profile assignments not only helped them strengthen their courage muscles and get comfortable with sharing their ideas to leaders across the organization, but also gave them visibility. Donofrio's message to them was to embrace their courage and to share their ideas broadly across the organization.

Colin Parris, CTO at GE Digital, remembers being a young employee at IBM, frustrated that he wasn't advancing in the organization despite his PhD and MBA. He went to Donofrio for advice. "Nick said, If you want to increase your visibility, go on some task forces as a side job." Parris agreed to the challenge, and Donofrio put him on two task forces he was running. "I began to [meet] other people in the company," Parris told me. "Pretty soon, a bunch of other people began to know my name—people in the systems group and people in the financial group. I got on slates of high-level execs only because they saw me in those task forces."

Like Parris, Ayna Agarwal, cofounder of she++, was lucky enough to have a senior leader who encouraged her to take risks when she began her career at Palantir Technologies. "My female manager was very supportive and forceful in a good way. She encouraged me to seize opportunities I would have otherwise never imagined for myself. She would say, 'I want to give you this responsibility. I want you to take on this project. I want you to solve this problem first,'" Agarwal shared with me. "That was honestly brilliant. In the early part of [your] career, I think you need to have an advocate like that to cultivate your fullest potential."

The approaches of Donofrio and of Agarwal's manager ensured that individuals who were making meaningful contributions had a chance to present their ideas. Creating a culture of courage is not about providing significant opportunities for those who are not ready yet. Instead, it's about regularly providing all of your employees chances—sometimes small, sometimes big—to demonstrate their courage. Doing so, however, will require that you challenge your biases and push beyond your comfort zone when you evaluate leadership opportunities.

Support Employees Who Speak Truth to Power

No act requires more courage than standing up to wrongdoing or to powerful leaders when you know they are wrong. It is not an easy choice. Many of us shy away from conflict and confrontation. Even when Otto, the engineer I told you about at the beginning of this chapter, disparaged me in front of my team at Malleable, I didn't confront him publicly as I should have. And that failure to act contributed to the erosion of the culture of courage I had helped nurture. To create such a culture, you must speak out against bad behavior and, perhaps just as important, recognize, stand with, and reward employees who do.

Over the years I have heard many stories from technical women who have endured inappropriate behavior and aggressions from their male colleagues. Sadly, this happens even more often than is reported, as nondisclosure agreements are (anecdotally, since few talk about them) common in the technology field. I have also watched perfectly competent leaders sit on the sidelines, unwilling to stand up for their staff. Many people have chosen to tell their stories at great cost to their personal and professional lives. And if you ask them why they decided to do it, many will tell you it's because they hope their experience will give courage to others going through similar struggles to speak up.

That was the case with Françoise Brougher, a former executive at Pinterest who we came across in chapter 1. When she was fired after speaking up about being subjected to sexist treatment, including being paid less than male colleagues, she decided to go public about it. "I wanted to tell people who worked in tech to be careful because bias still happens in tech, despite all this effort [to diversify the culture] and all this recruiting," she told me in an interview. "I wanted to tell the world that even when you think you made it, and you are at the executive level, and you think you can change the culture, you are still a victim of discrimination."

Brougher felt that she was in a good place to speak up. She didn't care about future roles, and having spent twenty-five years in tech, she felt credible. So, she wrote a blog post detailing how she was mistreated at Pinterest and fired for bringing it up. To her surprise, more than 250,000 people read her post. Since then, she's heard from many women in similar situations who've told her companies are more willing to settle in private to avoid having their stories in the media. However, that's not what Brougher wants.

"What I want is more women in executive positions," she explained. "I care that we mentor, train, and give them a chance to become executives. That's what I want." Before she sat down with Pinterest to settle her lawsuit, she made an agreement conditional on the fact that she was not going to sign a nondisclosure agreement. She intended to make public whatever settlement they agreed on. "I care about impact," Brougher told me. "I wanted people, other women, to say, 'Look, she got this, I need to get my share.' Discrimination exists."

Brougher became a role model for many women by going public. She received significant positive feedback from her colleagues, but also from the broader technology community.

When you are committed to a culture of courage, it is important to create an environment where your employees are willing to report serious issues and feel heard. You cannot create a culture of courage if you don't take their feedback seriously, listen, and respond. Although the HR department should be supportive when issues of harassment and discrimination are reported, the CEO and other executives set the tone for acceptable behavior. In times when your team is aware of an issue in their ranks, how you talk about courage and your beliefs in the importance of speaking up can impact both the immediate situation and how your entire team sees your commitment to the culture.

My first technical job was at the UNIVAC division of Sperry, a computer company that once was an IBM rival. The site manager regularly told the female employees that they needed to sleep with him to keep their jobs. He didn't follow through on his threat, and there were enough of us that we banded together to keep him at bay. But the technical leaders did not do anything about his behavior, even though they were well aware of his actions. Thinking back on how this behavior was normalized and accepted is horrifying.

While sexual harassment may not always be as overt today, it remains disturbingly common, as the #MeToo movement revealed. In my survey of technical people and people of color, 12 percent of the women and a whopping 27 percent of Latinas who responded reported being sexually harassed. Anecdotally, almost 100 percent of the women in technology I know well—in addition to many, many more I've talked to through my work as an advocate of women in tech—have shared about being harassed. They've mentioned comments about their personal appearance, crass jokes, sexually explicit emails, oblique references to their leaving when they get married, and sexual rumors and unwelcome sexual advances. Many have had soul-leeching experiences.

"Six weeks into my internship, one of my fellow interns felt it was OK to show up at my door drunk and proposition me," an Asian software engineer responded to a question in the survey. "I was young (only nineteen at the time), living away from home, and was sh*t-scared. And because there were no guidelines and I was afraid of being looked at as the intern who reported sexual harassment, I never reported that incident. Safe to say, I didn't join that company when I got a full-time offer."

For many employees of color in tech, harassment can be subtle—but that doesn't make it any less damaging. A young Latina engineer told me that, when she joined a new company, she was treated with disrespect and condescension. In the previous round of layoffs, all the engineers from underrepresented groups had been let go. Her new boss made it clear that if she wasn't careful, she would be next.

Many women and people of color I've spoken to over the years have told me that sexual and racial harassment and other improper behavior often go unaddressed—or worse, are protected. A white female tech lead shared that she was harassed at her previous company. "Though I reported it to human resources and my manager's manager on multiple occasions . . . it was humiliating and degrading," she wrote. "He was never disciplined." A female senior technical manager told me that when she reported that a colleague was harassing her, her boss was furious. "He said, 'You're going to hurt this guy's career. This guy is very promising,'" she said. Since she was senior to the colleague harassing her, her boss thought her career would be fine. "[This] was not the reaction I expected because he had been a wonderful boss and mentor." She went to the head of the department, who removed her from that chain of command. Still, there was no resolution. "They ended up not doing anything," she told me. "There was an investigation, and they said it was a 'he said, she said' situation. If you haven't experienced one of these things, you don't realize how horrible that phrase is."

Personally, several women have confided in me that they have reported harassment to their companies. Without exception, reporting the unacceptable behavior had disastrous consequences for them. Managers ignored their complaints or required them to continue interacting with their aggressor on a regular basis. When an employee pushes through their fear and shows courage by bringing up an incident of harassment or mistreatment with leadership and HR, ignoring it or sweeping it under the rug sends a clear message: *Don't take risks; we don't have your back. Unless, of course, you are a rock star.*

One of the challenges in tech cultures is the belief that a few superstars are responsible (and revered) for generating the most important technological innovations in an organization. This bedrock belief causes some leaders and human resources staff to protect these "lone geniuses," usually men, at all costs. If one of them engages in inappropriate actions—whether it's sexual harassment or behavior that's sexist, racist, ableist, homophobic, or otherwise offensive—they are often let off the hook. The perception that their technical skills are essential to the organization trumps whatever momentum there is to deal with their transgressions.

An Asian survey respondent captured this clearly when she reported that, in her experience at two companies, it is common for leadership to "acknowledge the obstacles, but *not* for superiors to speak to their difficult employees about correcting their behavior, either because they feel it will not change anything or they feel that the employee has a personal excuse that explains their behavior." Like many other people from underrepresented groups, she wants this to change. "I hope that future generations of female engineers will enter the workforce in a culture that is less tolerant of hostile, ego-driven behavior, and better champion collaboration and mutual respect," she wrote. Technical women everywhere join her in that hope.

If an employee has the courage to speak up about receiving mistreatment of any kind, do the following:

1. Listen to them with compassion and respect.

2. Summon the courage to stand up and call out inappropriate behavior, making clear that it is not tolerated in your organization.

3. Ensure that there are consequences for the aggressor and that the person will not engage in the behavior again at your organization—whether that means requiring they attend training and counseling or, if necessary, firing them.

4. Take actions to heal any damage the person caused, such as reviewing or reconsidering the effect that the behavior might have had on the affected employee and their record or reviews.

As a leader of an organization, I urge you to consider carefully—especially if you are male—how you receive harassment reports. I strongly support creating paths for employees to report problems anonymously, as long as there is a process for ensuring that the reports are followed up on. Some large companies, for example, deploy anonymous phone lines staffed by outside parties that vet reports, but still guarantee action on them. Smaller organizations can set up email accounts where employees can send confidential reports. Understand that you may not hear about some of the egregious behavior your employees encounter. But the way you communicate your organization's willingness to receive reports can encourage people to speak up.

The link between innovation and demonstrating the courage to speak truth to power may not seem obvious. But they are deeply intertwined. As innovators, our job is to come up with ideas for new ways of doing and thinking about something, and to risk failure. Knowing that our bosses and our organizations have our backs—that they care for our contributions and will not put up with anyone who shuts down the candid and respectful exchange of ideas—brings out the best in us. It emboldens us to experiment and bring our perspectives to the table—however how wild they might be. Because many breakthroughs started as wild ideas.

Loud in the Best Possible Way

Erica Lockheimer is a first-generation college graduate who worked almost full-time while studying computer engineering at San José State University. For many years, she was vice president of engineering at LinkedIn. As she advanced in her career, the leaders she worked for encouraged her to take risks. And she was not shy about speaking up. "I was a loud person with a loud voice," she told me. "I would raise my voice about how I wanted things to be." Above all, she gained the courage to speak up and advocate for herself.

After years of working at LinkedIn, she found herself evaluating work opportunities based on what her kids and family needed from her. She decided to be more intentional about her career, so that her work time was spent on projects that mattered to her. "I sought advice from our former CEO," she explained. "I told him [about] my dream job. I like working on something that's going to impact the world. And that means helping people learn, helping people get jobs; that makes me feel excited. His advice was to write it down and ask for it. I decided to raise my hand." She asked to run LinkedIn Talent Solutions, LinkedIn Learning, *and* Glint, an employee voice survey platform the company had recently acquired. The three lines of businesses combined had a nine-hundred-person team and were worth over $9 billion in revenue. At first her boss believed the role was too large, but to her surprise, he told her the company had considered her proposal and agreed. "Sometimes, you've got to fight." Lockheimer observed that it's also critical to have allies. "Allies were rooting for me and influencing the decision even when I was not in the room," she said. Lockheimer leveraged her leadership position to create a culture of courage within her organization and found ways for her entire team to accept more significant roles and to take risks. Many people, particularly women, consider her a mentor and have found their own courage through her coaching.

Some people, like Lockheimer, naturally have courage built into their souls and fight for what they want. They are "loud" in the best possible way—not afraid to speak up or share their risky ideas and ambitions. Technology companies need people like her.

By fostering a culture of courage, you can create an organization where those people abound. In fact, as you systematically promote courage, ideas and innovations will surface from many people who may not have had a chance to shine yet. One of those ideas could change your company or the world. Listen.

ACTIONS

To create a culture of courage, create an environment where employees feel empowered to take risks and speak truth to power.

Create Opportunities for All Employees to Contribute

Intentionally and systematically invite everyone to share their ideas. Host forums, hackathons, and discussion sessions for employees to present new and novel perspectives and discuss new product and feature ideas. Make sure your organization's leaders encourage participation and conversations to ensure all voices are heard.

Actively call on employees who are not participating. Notice who is not speaking, and contemplate why. Consider the informal norms for participating in meetings, and challenge them when they are preventing some employees from speaking up. Follow up offline with those who may not enjoy being called out in big meetings, asking for their ideas.

Recognize and praise employees when they offer new and novel approaches. When someone speaks up and makes a suggestion, acknowledge it by repeating the idea with attribution and thanking them. Recognize that most ideas in their final form were created from multiple inputs and through much iteration, so be sure to recognize contributions from all who provide them.

Normalize vulnerability. Discuss business and technical issues that you are grappling with or are unsure about with your team. Seek their advice and help to resolve them. Make a point of talking about and analyzing failures so employees know they can learn from them.

Assign High-Risk, High-Reward Assignments Broadly

Review your organization's methodology for assigning important projects or membership on critical task forces. Understand and evolve your own approach to assignments to ensure a broad set of projects reach a diverse pool of recipients.

Communicate future projects and potential task forces. Let all your employees know about projects on the horizon or task forces that contribute to your organization's future, so they have time to put their names in the hat to join them.

Challenge managers to provide all employees with opportunities to take risks. Ask managers and leaders what they are doing to help employees push themselves beyond their comfort zones and to grow the next generation of talent.

Support Employees Who Speak Truth to Power

Support and communicate your appreciation of challenging feedback. Acknowledge how hard it is for employees, especially those from underrepresented groups, to speak their truth. Encourage everyone to call out problems when they see them, and create safe spaces for them to do so, such as confidential hotlines.

Take those who speak up seriously. Listen to their concerns with compassion and respect. Ensure that *all* reports of harassment are reported through the proper channels. Track what happens after harassment is reported to you or to HR.

Commit to holding all employees accountable for their behavior, regardless of rank. Call out inappropriate behavior and make clear it is not tolerated from anyone. Make sure there are consequences for those who behave inappropriately—no matter what value their skills bring to the company.

‹4›
CONFIDENCE

After a while, I developed internal confidence. I'm here because I'm capable. . . . I worked extremely hard to be here and deserve the promotion.

—Li Fan, CTO, Circle; former CTO, Lime; and head of engineering, Pinterest

At Actel I was considered to be an up-and-coming leader by many. While I remember the warm glow of the spotlight, I also remember the many times I heard the explicit message that I had received recognition only because I was a woman. It stung. Rumors circulated about how overly ambitious I was. And a few people speculated about the "real" reason I had been promoted (it couldn't possibly have been my performance). My promotion had come on the heels of the successful launch of an important software release. But I was still young, and the group I was heading was new. Although intellectually I knew that what fueled this whisper campaign was jealousy, insecurity, and bias—on the part of not only male leaders but also a few women who had been conditioned to think of women getting leadership roles as a zero-sum game—the gossip fueled my fears and self-doubts. I questioned my ability to deliver the results Actel needed to survive. I wondered if I could do the job.

Actel didn't offer leadership training, so I enrolled in a new mentoring program in the Bay Area. As part of the program, I met monthly with a successful female CEO who ran a software company. I can still remember those meetings vividly. In our walks on the Baylands in Palo Alto, she shared with me her journey and encouraged me to develop resilience. When we wrapped up our yearlong engagement, she arranged an informational interview with each of her executive staff members, which provided me with insight into the mindsets and practices of successful executives. In large part due to her mentorship, I went on to make smart decisions at Actel that resulted in success for the company, including developing an exceptional logic synthesis capability for customers to use with its main product.

My mentor helped me see something in myself that I had lost sight of: confidence in my abilities, skills, and judgment. I will forever be grateful for her help.

Confidence is an elusive quality. It's the belief in one's ability to succeed or to accomplish a specific task. It makes us feel empowered and at ease in our skin. When we are confident, we are comfortable expressing our ideas, taking risks, and pursuing our goals because we trust we have the skills and strength to navigate whatever comes our way. If you exude confidence, you are more likely to be heard and trusted.

Yet you need to develop courage *before* you can develop confidence. That's because courage is about acting in the face of fear or danger, like a hostile environment. Confidence, on the other hand, has to do with how you feel about your ability to accomplish a task or goal. For example, you need to have the courage to speak up in a meeting—that is, to face the fear of being ignored or dismissed, which for people from underrepresented groups is not a "perceived" fear but a consequence of working in an environment that does not feel welcoming. But you also need the *confidence* to speak up—the belief that what you have to say is valuable and will be heard in good faith by others.

Confidence should not be confused with extroversion. You can be outgoing, high-energy, and talkative, and still lack confidence. And you can be introverted, reserved, and a person of few words, and be very confident. These kinds of distinctions are important precisely because the lens of the dominant culture so often determines how we perceive confidence. In the United States we often associate it with certain traits, behaviors, and styles of communication that are aligned with white, male, and Western cultural norms. This often leads us to perceive people of underrepresented groups as unconfident simply because their demeanor is different. For example, a young woman from certain parts of Asia may be less direct in her communication style or more reserved in her interactions. And yet, she might be quite secure in her skills and knowledge.

A culture of confidence is essential for fostering innovation. Innovation involves taking risks which requires courage, as we explored in chapter 3, and a strong belief that we can tackle any obstacle. Confidence also helps people bounce back from setbacks and failures, which are inevitable in the pursuit of innovation. In a culture of confidence, team members trust one another's abilities, leading to positive collaboration. Additionally, they are brave enough to take ownership of their work. When team members feel secure in their skills and are given a chance to pursue their ideas, they are inspired to push the boundaries. Fostering a culture of confidence encourages *all* team members to contribute their best, breaking down barriers and promoting inclusivity in the process. Creating a culture of confidence requires:

- Setting clear and fair expectations

- Paying attention to the confidence levels of your team members

- Promoting allyship and sponsorship across the organization

- Ensuring there is a diverse group of role models in your organization

To create a culture of confidence, you must be intentional about it. You can't just hire confident people and cross it off your list. Even if you did, what happens inside your organization will determine whether these hires remain that way, or whether their confidence is either tamped down or dominates others.

The Silent Innovation Killer

Fostering confidence is critical to tech organizations because their current environments and cultures are breeding grounds for impostor syndrome, a psychological phenomenon where people doubt their abilities despite having ample evidence of their competence and success. They fear being exposed as inadequate even though they may be highly accomplished—a fear I'm familiar with, as I described at the beginning of this chapter. Impostor syndrome is most often associated with women, but in my experience tech employees of all genders are susceptible to it. In fact, research has found that it disproportionally affects high-achieving people, and some informal studies have identified tech workers as some of the most affected.[1]

Tech cultures are fast-paced and high-pressure environments with tight deadlines, demanding workloads, and a constant push for results. Even in companies where collaboration is valued, the myth of the lone genius often perpetuates the idea that innovation is primarily driven by individual brilliance and talent. When I worked at Malleable, many in the company's leadership revered an engineer who was technically brilliant. He worked night and day on a key module for our main product and was held up to the team as a genius. Many employees felt insecure that they didn't work as much as he did and even doubted their technical skills in the face of his unique impact on a core piece of our software system.

Over time, though, I noticed this engineer made an increasing number of mistakes. He was not taking advantage of industry-standard algorithms that others in his area of expertise relied on, and, frankly, he wasn't getting enough sleep, affecting his performance. In the long run, while his ideas were still brilliant, he did not implement them effectively, and he was only modestly successful. For many so-called lone geniuses in the computing industry, this is not an unusual outcome. But even if a tech team has an exceptional performer who, unlike my former colleague, always delivers, research has found that a group of collaborators will likely do better than that person alone when working on complex problems. Collaboration almost always delivers more impactful results; one person's technical brilliance can deliver only so much value.[2]

Tech organizations where people like my former colleague are revered can make employees feel they must constantly prove their worth, live up to unrealistic standards, and strive for perfection. The fact that lone geniuses are put on a pedestal and are considered above all rules by management suggests, tacitly, that others should copy their behavior, including their workaholism. Employees, then, believe they must compare themselves with these star performers, and when they perceive themselves as falling short, they feel inadequate. Since computer science evolves incredibly fast, with new technologies and methodologies constantly emerging, people in technical roles also feel pressure to stay up-to-date and continuously expand their skills to remain relevant and come up with the next big thing. While this can be intellectually stimulating, it can also be daunting and lead to feelings of self-doubt when engineers are confronted with particularly challenging problems.

On top of dealing with the self-doubt common among the high-achieving population in tech companies, imagine if you are an only being told—over and over again—you do not belong or that you are only there because the bar was lowered. How likely would you be to internalize those messages? Members of underrepresented groups already must deal with what social scientists call *stereotype threat*—the risk that, when anxious about performing as is expected of them, the anxiety negatively affects their performance in ways that confirm the very stereotypes that they are trying to prove wrong in the first place.[3] When the standards for performance are unrealistically set by lone geniuses, the risk is that much higher.

In short, cultures that lionize star talent can unwittingly pressure employees to appear "strong" and "successful" at all times. They contribute to environments where performative workaholism, avoidance of vulnerability, and resistance to collaboration prevail. They kill confidence—and innovation.[4] Creating a culture where confidence can manifest in many different ways (not just bravado or extroversion) can help reduce the prevalence of impostor syndrome, bolster innovation, and encourage more inclusive workplaces and communities. It can also counter the idea that members of underrepresented groups must "fix themselves"—meaning that if they are not thriving, it's probably because they lack confidence, rather than because the environment in which they are expected to perform needs to change.

How We Perceive Confidence in Others

While confidence is vital to a healthy tech organization, leaders need to remember it is a double-edged sword. Internally, you know whether you have the belief that you can succeed and handle a task. But detecting confidence in others is not as easy. We think we will know it when we see it. But how we perceive it in others is shaped by stereotypes and biases.

In particular, many traits we associate with confidence are traditionally perceived as masculine: assertiveness, decisiveness, self-assuredness, charisma, independence, and self-reliance. When exhibited by people from underrepresented groups, these characteristics are not always seen as positives. For example, if Black employees exhibit them, they may be perceived as aggressive or angry. If women do, they can be accused of being bold, bossy, overly ambitious, or selfish. In a recent study, Laura Guillen and her colleagues at INSEAD found that for many women, believing in their self-confidence did not translate to being *perceived* as confident.[5]

While women and other employees from underrepresented groups pay a steep price for this bias, so do organizations. When someone is perceived as confident, we listen to them, believe them, and trust their competence. But if people are shut down because they are not seen as confident, organizations risk losing their contributions. Tech leaders fostering a culture of confidence not only need to help individuals feel genuinely capable of tackling the hard work in front of them, but must also put significant effort into ensuring bias is not baked into these kinds of perception, shutting out the very voices who might bring fresh perspectives.

Set Clear and Fair Expectations

A meaningful way to increase confidence among your tech workforce is to have clear performance and promotion standards. Uncertainty and ambiguity about expectations and promotion often lead to feelings of anxiety and self-doubt among all employees.

When people understand what is expected of them and what they need to do to succeed, they feel more confident in their ability to perform well. It's a lot easier to believe in your abilities to do something when you know what that something is. Clear expectations also provide people with clear goals and benchmarks. With tangible goals to work toward, they feel empowered to take ownership of their jobs and opportunities to move up the ladder, which leads to more confidence in their ability to get it done right.

More importantly, having clear standards helps ensure fairness and transparency in performance evaluations and promotion decisions. When success criteria are clearly defined and consistently applied, employees feel confident that their work will be evaluated fairly and that promotions will be based on objective rather than subjective factors. Studies have shown, for example, that women often have to prove themselves through performance while men only have to show potential to be promoted.[6] Clear success criteria can also dispel assumptions that the performance bar is lower for members of an underrepresented group who are assumed to be employed as "diversity hires"—not for their talents or potential.

From the survey I conducted in 2021, it's clear women and other tech workers from some underrepresented groups don't feel they know what it takes to advance in their companies. Fifty-two percent of the men said they believed they understood what it took to advance compared to thirty-six percent of women, thirty-five percent of Black, and thirty-eight percent of Asian respondents. This might explain the finding in McKinsey's "Women in the Workplace" study that for every one hundred men who were promoted, only eighty-seven women and seventy-three women of color were promoted.[7]

When asked what companies could do to promote inclusive environments, many survey respondents noted the need for better standards and feedback. "Provide clear guidance on advancement criteria," a white female software engineer offered. "Increase transparency, particularly around promotion and compensation," wrote an Asian female account executive.

In a landmark study, Shelley Correll, a professor of organizational behavior at Stanford University, and her associates found that gender bias often creeps into the evaluations of women. "Where we find the bigger biases are in evaluations of people's personalities, their future potential, and on the mentions of exceptionalism," Correll told Insights by Stanford Business.[8] The criteria for success in tech roles can be ambiguous and subjective, particularly in areas such as leadership and innovation. This ambiguity creates opportunities for bias to affect performance evaluations, as managers may rely on personal preferences or stereotypes.

Especially when it comes to leadership roles, "top jobs are given to those who also look and act the part, who manifest 'executive presence,'" explains Sylvia Ann Hewlett, the founder of the Center for Talent Innovation, in an article for hbr.org. "Yet because senior leaders are overwhelmingly Caucasian, professionals of color (African American, Asian, and [Latine] individuals) find themselves at an immediate disadvantage in trying to look, sound, and act like a leader."[9] All too often, I've heard from people from underrepresented groups who are denied promotions or leadership opportunities because they lack "leadership presence" or "need to work on their confidence." They were looked past, not considered for promotions, only to see less experienced and less accomplished male colleagues being given those opportunities. The problem, however, is rarely with employees' confidence or leadership potential, but more with arbitrary promotion processes that don't evaluate employees on the same criteria. Unless companies set clear, consistent expectations, baked-in biases that plague often-relied-on qualities for determining traits such as "leadership presence" will continue to disqualify deserving talent.

As you evolve your culture, remember that recognizing your team members' achievements goes a long way toward encouraging their confidence. Providing clear performance expectations reduces uncertainty about the fairness of the evaluation process. It allows all team members to focus their energy and efforts on collaborating and getting their work done. By establishing clear standards, you can boost the confidence of everyone on your team, empowering them to perform at their best and achieve their full potential.

Pay Attention to the Confidence Levels of Your Team Members

Setting clear expectations helps give your employees a direction to aim for. But along the way, people often encounter obstacles or experience setbacks that may shake their belief in their abilities and competence. Leaders must pay close attention to their employees' confidence levels and act to bolster them.

To build confidence in their teams, great leaders help their employees see the value of what they've contributed. They publicly give them appropriate credit for their ideas and document their achievements in performance reviews. Some companies are moving away from formal performance reviews, but great leaders provide regular and ongoing feedback that is concrete, thorough, and actionable. Leaders in any organization should do this. But since technical staff are evaluated primarily on their technological achievements, their leaders must especially help them develop the confidence to own their ideas and the skills to articulate their impact.

Alan Eustace, who spent many years at Google as vice president of search before retiring, was well-known for paying attention to his employees. Eustace worked with my dear friend Anita Borg at a Digital Equipment Corporation research lab in Palo Alto in the 1980s and '90s. Her vision to achieve a tech workforce that was at least 50 percent women profoundly influenced his thinking. She taught him what was possible if women were given a chance, and this experience shaped his perspective as he became an executive, first as director of the Western Research Laboratory and then at Google, where he held various positions, including senior vice president of engineering.

Stu Feldman, a legendary Unix technologist from Bell Labs and a former technology executive at IBM, worked for Eustace at Google. He told me Eustace once asked why women were not going up for promotions, and was told that it was likely because they were afraid to fail. Eustace didn't buy it. Instead, he emailed all the women on the team, asking them to consider going up for promotion. "If you have a chance, you should because you'll get some good comments, even if you don't make it the first time," he wrote to them. Suddenly, the percentage of women candidates getting promoted increased and was about the same as the percentage of men.

With this small act, Eustace sent the message to the women on his team that he believed in them and that even if they didn't receive a promotion, they should give it a try and learn from the experience. He recognized that encouragement mattered for those who felt like one of a few. In my interviews, many women described Eustace's positive impact on their careers, including a growing confidence in their abilities.

Raquel Romano, a former technical leader at Google, was one of the women who put themselves forward for a promotion because of those emails. "I always defaulted to waiting and thinking that I had a lot of work to do before I was ready for a promotion," she explained to me. "It was beneficial to hear from trusted voices that I should apply for a promotion." Romano was surprised when her promotion was approved. I suspect Eustace wasn't.

Keeping an eye on people's confidence, like he did, allows you to identify who in your organizations most needs a confidence boost. But leaders would do well to keep an eye especially on employees from underrepresented groups. As Romano so eloquently describes, if you are an only on a team, there is a particular benefit to being encouraged. While holding leadership roles at several tech startups and a nonprofit, I had a front-row seat to seeing people from underrepresented groups rise to the challenge when I encouraged them to take on additional responsibility.

Promote Allyship and Sponsorship Across the Organization

As Eustace's story suggests, having someone believe in you is instrumental to believing in your ability to succeed. Many men who deeply care about their colleagues, such as Eustace, find ways to be influential allies and sponsors.

An ally actively supports underrepresented groups, recognizes the systemic barriers and biases they face, and takes intentional action to promote equity. Allies can come from all organizational levels—you don't have to be a manager or a leader. They use their platform and influence to amplify the voices and ideas of individuals from underrepresented groups. They promote their work, report their achievements, and highlight their expertise in meetings, presentations, and even informal gatherings. They interrupt microaggressions when they see them and challenge stereotypes and bias. And they create a supportive environment by actively offering encouragement and validation. With these intentional actions, allies play a critical role in supporting a culture of confidence.[10]

To encourage allyship in your organization, there are a number of actions that Karen Catlin suggests in her book *Better Allies*:[11]

- Ask for input from the technologists of underrepresented groups in your organization. Listen to, acknowledge, and validate their points of view, even if you've never personally experienced what they are describing.

- Speak up if you witness discriminatory (sexist, racist, homophobic, ableist, and so on) behavior or comments.

- Call out gaslighting by other team members.

- Share or cede the spotlight to a technologist of an underrepresented group.

Sponsorship is also crucial to fostering confidence at the individual level. Unlike mentors, who provide guidance and advice, or allies, who focus on broader systemic change to address harmful behavior and promote inclusion, sponsors take a more active role in promoting their protégés, leveraging their influence and networks to open doors and create opportunities for them. Janice Omadeke, the CEO of The Mentor Method, which builds software to facilitate mentorship connections, explains that a sponsor helps their protégé get visibility in the organization: "For instance, a sponsor may put their protégé's name on the table for a promotion or have the power to advocate for their work when they are not in the room (or invited to the 'important' meeting themselves). The sponsor puts their reputation and professional branding behind the protégé, meaning there's typically more risk to being a sponsor."[12]

Sponsorship has been around for as long as people have worked in skilled trades. Historically, apprenticeships provided a path to learning a trade and offered job opportunities. But today, leaders in companies are more likely to informally adopt up-and-coming talent and find opportunities for them. The problem is that all too often, in male-dominated industries like tech, leaders tend to gravitate toward sponsoring others who have backgrounds and experiences similar to their own. They may hold unconscious biases that favor these team members or that fit traditional stereotypes of success, leading to informal sponsorship mostly of other men like them. Some leaders may perceive advocating for a person from a marginalized group as riskier or outside their comfort zones. That may lead to a preference for advocating for individuals perceived as lower risk, such as other white men.

Informal sponsorship often relies on networks and relationships built through informal channels such as sporting events, social gatherings, networking events, and mentorship programs. Employees from underrepresented groups may have difficulty accessing these networks of influential leaders, limiting their opportunities to find sponsors organically. That's where formal sponsorship programs come in. These programs match leaders in the organization with talented members of underrepresented groups, creating a more even playing field for them. Knowing that senior leaders have identified them as high potentials boosts these employees' belief in their capabilities and their future within the organization. It also gives them a sense of validation and recognition for their skills and abilities, which is particularly important during times of uncertainty or adversity. In my work, I've learned the best results come when *all* senior leaders in the organization are expected to be sponsors and ensure a diverse set of people are sponsored.

Although the term *sponsor* is common to describe these roles, some people strongly prefer *advocate,* including Diane Bryant. Bryant was a senior executive at Intel for many years before taking the CEO role at medical technology firm NovaSignal. She's a fierce proponent of advocacy—particularly for those who are unfairly blocked from key opportunities. In 2004, Bryant was promoted to vice president at Intel. At an event celebrating her promotion, she was shocked to learn that only 14 of the 250 vice presidents were women. Those women decided the situation had to change. They created an advocacy program: they would each identify two other women who they believed had what it took to become vice presidents but had been unfairly overlooked year after year, and would actively advocate for them until they were promoted.

Bryant shared with me, "For example, I knew someone who was an outstanding leader and critical to the company. So when the next nomination process started and her manager failed to nominate her, I intercepted his submission of nominees. I told him, 'Please explain to me why you are not nominating this person for vice president. What capabilities is she lacking relative to the men you are nominating?'" The manager was taken off guard by the question and didn't have an answer. In the end, he decided to nominate this person, and she was promoted.

Bryant and the other women vice presidents were able to leverage their senior positions and influence effectively. "Our group challenged the system and applied pressure for as many years as it took to get the deserving women they had identified promoted," she said. Once they succeeded, all the women vice presidents—including those recently promoted—would identify two more qualified women and restart the process.

"We went from six percent of the vice presidents being women in 2004 to 21 percent by 2015," Bryant told me. "In eleven years, the women at Intel became visible leaders, sitting at the executive table with true corporate power and influence."

Jennifer Chayes, a longtime research executive at Microsoft who transitioned to a role as dean of the College of Computing,

Data Science, and Society at the University of California, Berkeley, also ensured that her technical staff, many of whom were women, received the consideration they deserved. "When I see a young woman, sometimes I realize she reminds me of me. And so that leads some young people to get more face time, and it can have a huge impact on their careers. When an executive hears a person who articulates a great idea, they might decide that this is good for their organization—'I will give this person a chance,'" she explained "I've always tried to advocate for my people, both men and women. Sometimes, I would believe the women I mentored were ready for a promotion. And I would express this to their manager, which was often unappreciated. However, I observed that my mentorship helped my mentees develop confidence."

In interview after interview, technologists have told me that being sponsored by a senior leader was instrumental to their success. Knowing that they had someone in their corner who was championing them gave them a shot of confidence, as they felt supported and valued within the organization. Brianna Fugate, a Black software engineer, told me the director of engineering at Mailchimp, where she worked at the time, took an interest in her success and sponsored her throughout her tenure.

"He is the definition of someone who comes from privilege: he's a white male. And yet he made me feel included; he made me feel like I had a place there," she told me. The executive introduced himself and told her to let him know if she needed anything. They started following each other on social media and eventually met for lunches. Although he was in a position of power, he always ended their conversations with this question: What can I do to help you? "The organic conversation and relationship were helpful because nothing was too much for me to ask of him," Fugate shared. "He genuinely wanted to help me.

"There are some people who go above and beyond to help you. I had one manager who supported me, encouraged me to do better, mentored me, and now, even though he does not work with me, he is in touch . . . [to check] if I am doing well, excelling in my career."

   —Asian woman, data scientist

"Taking the time to touch base regularly is important, and my supervisors (all of whom have been male) are quick/eager to give me advice and suggestions on how I can improve."

   —Latina, computer systems analyst

"I received a mentor in my sophomore year of my undergraduate studies. Eleven years later, she is still my mentor. We have the same race and gender. She got me my first and only civil engineering–related internship the summer after my sophomore year. She got me my first job after graduating with my master's. She got me my second job after leaving the first. Out of all of my attempts to obtain an internship or full-time employment, I only received one offer in a seven-year period."

   —Black woman, civil engineer

"I have to prove every time that I have technical depth, as opposed to my male peers [who don't have to]. This erodes your self-confidence over time."

   —Asian woman, software engineer

Having a sponsor was critical. He's done this for other people who look like me at my company and has impacted what engineering there looks like."

I know firsthand the value of having a sponsor who instills confidence in you. Over the years, I've had the good fortune to have several sponsors. But my most impactful one was Carver Mead. As a graduate student at Caltech, I was painfully aware of being one of the few women working in the field. At the time, Mead, a person many consider the father of VLSI design, was my PhD adviser. I trusted him precisely because he was deeply committed to the science and did not get caught up in people's politics. How we partnered together helped me develop confidence and a deep belief in my work. Mead had connections to people I did not know and trusted my ability to contribute. After I graduated, he did what any good sponsor does, and put his reputation on the line when he connected me to the leadership of the research lab and the two startups where I spent the first half of my career. In 2022 I was elected to the National Academy of Engineering, and I believe Mead's recommendation was critical to the academy's decision. Throughout my career, I've benefited greatly from his advocacy.

Most of the senior executives I interviewed told me their relationships with sponsors happened organically, as they did for Fugate and me. Some companies have created formal programs to accelerate the confidence-building and inclusivity-promoting benefits of sponsorship. One example of such a program was at Uber, which became infamous in 2017 for its poor treatment of women employees after a whistleblower, Susan Fowler, wrote an exposé about the company in a blog post.[13] But sometimes the worst offenders are the most committed to creating change after a leadership change.

Thuan Pham was the CTO of Uber at the time, and he remained after its CEO was fired. Before leaving for a position at Coupang, Pham launched a formal sponsorship program. He and his leadership team identified talented individuals from underrepresented groups, then they solicited sponsors among the engineering ranks. Through a matching process, sponsors and talent were paired up to go through a four-month program. "The explicit agreement is that the sponsorship relationship is far more profound than a mentoring relationship. It's about looking at that person, looking at that person's arc, and seeing where that person could potentially prosper," Pham told me. "We see the opportunities, and sometimes we push and create the opportunity. We open that door and that path for that person to go through."

Pham remembers hosting the program's first graduating class in San Francisco not too long before the Covid-19 shutdown. "People were buzzing," he told me. Those matched with a sponsor were thankful to have them in their corner, to have someone advocating for them and raising their confidence.

Sponsorship programs like the one Thuan developed do far more than raise the confidence of those being sponsored—they often result in meaningful career opportunities, especially when sponsors remain invested over the long term. The aim is ultimately to provide employees from underrepresented groups with opportunities for growth that are already commonly available, even if informally, for many from majority populations. I passionately believe that fostering a culture of confidence has to include providing opportunities for *all* talented employees to find sponsors. So take time to examine your selection process to eliminate any biases in your sponsorship decisions and make sure all your employees—people from all backgrounds—have the support they need to increase their confidence and achieve their highest potential.

Ensure There Is a Diverse Group of Role Models in Your Organization

Growing up, I was unconsciously drawn to strong female role models even when I didn't understand what a role model was. I had no exposure to female scientists or technologists. But I followed Martina Navratilova's and Billie Jean King's careers, not because I was interested in tennis but because they embodied a competitive female spirit. Later in my life, Sally Ride, the first American woman to fly in space, inspired me. (I was blessed to meet her during my early days at AnitaB.org.) As a child, though, most people I aspired to emulate were men. They had the power.

Role models provide inspiration and aspiration. Seeing that someone who looks like us or shares our experiences has achieved success can encourage us to believe in our potential, raise our confidence, and help us feel seen, understood, and valued. Observing how role models navigate challenges, make decisions, and interact with others also imparts valuable lessons and insights, especially when it comes to taking risks, pursuing brave new lines of thinking, and overcoming obstacles with greater resilience.

But while role models are essential to a culture of confidence and innovation, the lack of employees from underrepresented groups in technical roles means finding leaders who look like them is almost impossible.

Natalia Rodriguez, who works at literacy advocacy firm Reading Reimagined, found computing somewhat late as an undergraduate. After college, she joined Codecademy and then Wikimedia Foundation. While she thrived in both places, she grappled with feedback that she should appear more confident. Recently, she told me she used to yearn for a mentor from a similar background and heritage, other Latine product managers who might help her in this respect. But she found them to be quite rare. "We are about 1 percent of the tech workforce," she lamented. As she focused on her performance and was promoted, she began to develop the confidence she needed to be successful at the organization.

Finding someone to look up to is challenging not just for entry-level employees but also for those at higher levels, as Li Fan, CTO at Circle and former CTO of Lime, told me. "I see few role models for me—people who are CTOs or heads of engineers," she said. "For example, I'm a first-generation immigrant: how many first-generation immigrants have climbed up? When I look up, how many women become CEOs? We have some, but very few. Finding models is harder for me. I want to be a role model for my daughter's generation."

Fan is correct that women CEOs of *Fortune* 500 companies are rare—yet even rarer are women CEOs who come from a technical background. Lisa Su, CEO of AMD, the Silicon Valley computer chip manufacturer, is one of the few. After earning her PhD at MIT and working for tech companies like Texas Instruments and IBM, she joined AMD in 2012 as a senior vice president and general manager of the global business units. She rose up the ranks and took over the helm in 2014, when the company was in serious trouble. Together with Mark Papermaster, the CTO and executive vice president for technology and engineering, she turned AMD around and made it one of today's most successful chip companies. For women in technology, Su is easily one of the most important role models of our generation.

But one is not enough.

For young people, looking at their company leadership and seeing people who look like them is very important. While leaders from the dominant groups can sponsor individuals from underrepresented groups and act as effective allies, having a role model is essential early in someone's career since they provide a road map for what's possible long before the person is promoted for the first time. In other words, role models instill confidence that they can succeed. *If there is no one to look up to,* someone may ask, *if no one else like me has climbed the ladder, what are the chances that I will?*

As you set out to build a culture of confidence that will endure, understand that you can only instill confidence in all employees if they see themselves represented. When the next generation of young people look at your organization, will they see leaders who look like them? What roles do these folks have? Many executives I know brag that they have women on their executive staff. Often, these are in HR or other roles with traditionally more women—not in technical roles. Are there female leaders in your *engineering* teams? Do you have executives in technical roles who are from underrepresented groups? Who delivers the presentations at all-hands meetings or engineering forums?

Young engineers may not always give feedback when they fail to see diverse representation around the organization. But they notice and often vote with their feet. That's why it is essential to consider carefully whose work you feature and who may become role models for your staff. While technical expertise will still be your key consideration, do not shy away from considering the many aspects of diversity, such as gender, race, sexuality, age, and ability. If there isn't enough diversity among your leaders, make clear that having it in the future is a priority for the organization. A commitment to developing confidence for all members of your team includes providing role models for all. If that is not possible, then ensure that the employees who may not find one within the company have access to one elsewhere.

For example, tech companies are increasingly sending their employees to gatherings that are specifically designed for members of underrepresented groups, such as the Grace Hopper Celebration, the Society for Women Engineers conference, the Women in Product Conference, the Tapia Conference, the AfroTech conference, the Society of Hispanic Professional Engineers conference, and the Advancing Indigenous People in STEM conference. There are also many online forums where employees can participate and hear from inspirational leaders. The key point is to regularly communicate the importance of role models to *all* employees, and your support for external opportunities where they might be exposed to them.

One of the core reasons for the success of the Grace Hopper Celebration over the years has been the presence of role models. For women who work on teams where they are the only woman, having the chance to listen to and meet extraordinary peers from many companies and universities is hugely impactful. If you are a Black computer science student, hearing from a Black senior executive can be mind-shifting. If you are a lesbian engineer, hearing from a widely successful leader who was once in your shoes reminds you that you aren't alone. And so on. These events provide opportunities for unscripted interactions, especially for underrepresented people who feel isolated in their teams. UC Berkeley's Jennifer Chayes told me the Grace Hopper Celebration had a significant impact on many of her mentees. The chance to meet other women and see the support of their leadership and executives provided the motivation for many participants to develop confidence in their abilities.

Building Confidence Is a Journey

Helping your team build confidence will lead to more robust innovation and inclusivity. Employees who are sure of their abilities are more likely to take risks and think outside the box.

They're more likely to explore new approaches, experiment with novel solutions, and push the boundaries of what is possible. They will collaborate more effectively with others, share their knowledge, contribute diverse perspectives, and work better across disciplines. They help create a positive and supportive environment where everyone feels valued, respected, and empowered to succeed.

However, building your team's confidence can also contribute to *your* personal growth and development. It can help you improve your communication skills; your ability to lead, mentor, and inspire others; and your relationships with them. Investing in your team members' success and well-being can create a positive ripple effect that enhances the overall dynamics and morale within the organization.

As a bonus, knowing that you have positively impacted someone's life and contributed to their personal growth and success is incredibly rewarding in and of itself.

Ashley Conard first attended the Grace Hopper Celebration when she was a freshman at DePauw University and was curious to learn more about computer science. Later, Conard shared the moment the conference changed her perspective on computing and what was possible—and my role in it. "You were on stage presenting an award [and helped me] realize that everyone has a piece of knowledge that helps them create a beautiful, personalized solution to a hard problem," she told me. "That's the reason I ended up taking my first real computer science course in school." Conard eventually graduated with a PhD in computer science and computational biology from Brown University and is now a biomedical computing researcher at Microsoft Research.

When she told me this story, I was surprised and touched. Before the conference, she'd had access to few women role models in tech. I was honored that just standing on that stage, I had inspired her to reach her goals and contributed to her self-confidence. But mostly, I was grateful. Like all of us, I've had and continue to have doubts—about my worthiness to be on that stage, my value in speaking at events, and the significance of my work. But that day, knowing I helped encourage someone to set and achieve challenging goals gave me a deep sense of fulfillment and satisfaction. Conard's appreciation was affirming. It helped boost my confidence, which in turn deepened my resolve in my work. Building confidence, after all, is a virtuous cycle.

ACTIONS

To create a culture of confidence, ensure that employees understand what is expected of them and provide a collaborative environment of help and support.

Set Clear and Fair Expectations

Make performance expectations clear. Provide employees with goals and benchmarks they understand. Make sure people know what is expected of them and what they need to do to succeed. Give all employees concrete guidance on how to advance.

Publish and consistently apply promotion criteria. Pay close attention to your published standards when making promotion decisions. Avoid assessing employees' potential through personality traits that are often highly gendered.

Pay Attention to the Confidence Levels of Your Team Members

Help your employees see the value of what they've contributed. Recognize people's achievements by acknowledging them in team meetings. Publicly give people credit for their ideas. Provide encouragement by holding a retrospective meeting after a launch or decision, to point out what early contributions had an impact or led to other ideas.

Identify individuals who need a confidence boost. Look for employees, especially those from underrepresented groups, who are qualified but are not putting themselves up for special tasks or promotion. Let them know you believe in their abilities and skills.

Promote Allyship and Sponsorship Across the Organization

Coach your staff to be allies. Discuss the role of allies in the success of your organization, highlighting examples and articulating their impact. Solicit feedback from underrepresented groups as to what they are looking for in allies. Encourage allies to call out microaggressions or biased behavior.

Encourage or require your leaders to be sponsors. Discuss the importance of sponsorship with the leaders in your organization. Encourage them to sponsor employees outside of their existing network and avoid sponsoring only employees who share the same background or experience. Ensure that *you* are sponsoring people and talking about the experience.

Create a formal sponsorship program. Review your sponsorship program's impact regularly. Solicit feedback from participants, leaders, and the employee resource groups in your organization about the effectiveness of the program. Follow the data and evaluate the effectiveness of the sponsorship program.

Ensure There Is a Diverse Group of Role Models in Your Organization

Identify role models within your company. Look for people across a wide spectrum of diversity. Provide visibility for these role models, especially to younger staff early in their careers.

Support external opportunities for staff to find role models. Send employees to conferences, local meetups, or virtual events where they might meet role models. Solicit advice from your staff as to the external events they would like to attend.

‹5›
CURIOSITY

[Diversity and inclusion] is a journey. You've got to be
curious, you've got to be all in, and you've got to work
together as a community.

—Vijay Anand, executive vice president, R&D, Apree Health

I n 1992, while I was still at Actel, I was connected with several
organizations advocating for women in the computing field.
A year earlier, the Computing Research Association (CRA),
which was dedicated to uniting industry, academia, and govern-
ment to advance research, had created a committee on the status
of women, called CRA-W.[1] Anita Borg and I were involved in many
discussions with them, often centered on exposing and righting
the sexism and bias women in computing face day after day. But
we felt something was missing. Just as it was important to focus
on what was going wrong, we also wanted to put a spotlight on
what was going right. We wanted to celebrate women's achievements in the field, and thus the annual Grace Hopper Celebration
of Women in Computing was born.

For the first few years the conference attracted about five hundred people, almost all women. The spirit of the gathering was
electric, conferring a feeling that we were not alone and that,

together, we could and would change (and already *were* changing) the world. We hosted speakers presenting thought-provoking
talks on critical research areas, discussions about controversial
topics, and panels of leaders from the technology industry. But we
called the event a *celebration* because one of its goals was to have
fun, especially through its legendary dance parties. For many
female undergraduates and graduate students, attending a conference where hundreds of women were focused on technology
was the norm, not the exception, was a foundational experience.

Soon, companies discovered they could recruit at the Grace
Hopper Celebration, and most of the new or relatively newer
ones—these were the days of Intel, Cisco, DEC, Unisys, and
Microsoft—did so. Initially, they sent small recruiting teams.
Curious about the best way to attract the attendees, they experimented with approaches and hired women from across the spectrum of the universities represented. Most companies talked to
any student who approached their booth or table.

Over time the conference grew, and by 2015 there were more
than 11,700 attendees; by 2023 the number grew to 30,000. The
National Science Foundation provided scholarship money for
students to attend, a tradition it maintained for many years, and
eventually most universities in the United States with computer science programs awarded scholarships for women students to go. An
extraordinary number of talented female students were showing
up—and the number of teams hungry to hire them increased too.

As competition for candidates heightened, so did the rigidness
of the recruiting processes, especially those of the largest, leading companies. They lost their curiosity for experimenting with
different approaches and settled into traditional strategies. They
started screening candidates ahead of time and only interviewed
those graduating from a handful of elite programs. Talented
students—many who had moved heaven and earth to attend the

Grace Hopper Celebration—were discouraged that they could not get an interview, let alone an internship. Although we were blessed to host young students from historically Black colleges and universities, minority-serving institutions, and large public university programs that attract women and people of color—such as DePauw University, the University of Utah, San José State University, and the University of Florida—they were not being considered, even as the programs they attended graduated great talent.

Big tech companies like Google and Meta have always favored graduates from well-known programs like those at Carnegie Mellon, Georgia Tech, MIT, Princeton, Cornell, and Stanford. But they were already recruiting on campus at these select schools. The Grace Hopper Celebration became another prong of an existing approach. A student from, say, Carnegie Mellon would be recruited both on campus and at the conference. However, a student from a public university in the Midwest did not have the luxury of an on-campus interview and could not secure one at the Grace Hopper Celebration. The number of women—especially women of color—graduating from elite schools was small, so companies fought each other over a tiny pool of candidates, likely restricting the number of positions they filled with women. These companies played it safe: they stuck to the approach that had worked for them before.

What was going on? Recruiters were not *curious* enough. They were failing to ask questions like, Where can we find new sources of talent in tech? They were failing to challenge assumptions about whether the best talent can *only* come from their preferred (and well-trodden) recruitment grounds or whether other programs might prepare people from diverse backgrounds in a better way. They were failing to look closely at the data in front of them; they were ignoring the results. If they had looked around the executive ranks of great tech companies, they would have found successful technology executives and leaders who have graduated from the University of Utah (where I received my undergraduate degree), the University of Florida, and community colleges—the same schools that were not being considered. Not curious enough about who attended the conference from programs they *didn't* typically target, they were missing out on great talent.

We all have an innate sense of curiosity that drives our understanding of the world. Curiosity is at the heart of innovation and is fundamental to the success of any tech company. It leads us to explore unusual ideas and perspectives, question assumptions, consider new approaches, experiment, and take risks. It drives our knowledge-seeking; it motivates us to look deeply into data to discover what it reveals. When we are curious, we listen closely and pay attention, so we're more likely to develop products that better meet customers' needs—even needs they don't know they have yet. Put simply, companies that nurture a culture of curiosity are more likely to develop robust solutions for problems.

They are also more likely to build an inclusive culture.

When we encourage *asking questions and challenging assumptions,* we are more likely to respect people who are different from us—to want to learn what they know, where they come from, and what perspectives they can add to our team or project. When we encourage *being open to new ideas and perspectives,* we are more likely to recognize and value the ideas others bring to the table, especially those ideas born from having had an experience different from ours. When we encourage *leaning into curiosity to solve problems*—especially people problems—we are more likely to closely examine others' unique situations and find approaches that better meet their needs.

We often think of curiosity as an innate personality trait, but that couldn't be further from the truth. In fact, it's a skill that can be developed and embraced throughout an organization. There are four key things you can encourage everyone to do to foster a culture of curiosity:

- Engage in continuous learning

- Collaborate with others across the organization

- Dig more deeply into problems

- Challenge assumptions of "how things are done"

A culture that embraces new ideas from a multitude of fields also encourages people with different backgrounds and life experiences to express their ideas—and, more importantly, to have their viewpoints heard. Curiosity-driven innovation and curiosity-driven inclusion are deeply intertwined.

How Curiosity Fuels Innovation and Inclusivity

While a spirit of curiosity and flexibility is common at the beginning of an enterprise, as a company gets larger—especially in tech—many factors conspire to stifle it, and the entrenchment of some approaches is all but inevitable. We start rejecting outside ideas or anything that seems different from "how we do things" or was not created by us. We divide our work into specialized roles and departments, creating silos that isolate us from different perspectives and ways of doing things. Above all, we resist change. As my hero Grace Hopper once said, "The most dangerous phrase in the language is 'We've always done it this way.'"

At Actel, the products we developed early in my career used a brand-new process and chip architecture to provide customers with chips they could program in their own labs, what were called field-programmable gate arrays (FPGAs). FPGAs allowed engineers to "fabricate" the chip in their labs in days rather than months.

At the time, these radical innovations were embraced. But Actel also embodied a classical engineering culture where there were painful divisions between hardware and software. Both groups were committed to doing their work as they had always done it. That made it very difficult for software engineers and chip designers to come together and talk about future possibilities. In the end, Actel was modestly successful. After going public in 1993, it was purchased by Microsemi in 2010.

My experience at the company seems like a distant past, but according to the tech leaders I interviewed for this book, many still experience these same problems. Fostering a culture of curiosity, one that counters our tendencies to do things "how we've always done them" or to become siloed in our approaches, might just be the ticket to keep the spark of innovation alive in your organization. This can be increasingly difficult in a large company, but great ideas can emerge from small, focused teams. As Cyril Bouquet, Jean-Louis Barsoux, and Michael Wade write in a 2018 *Harvard Business Review* article, "To produce a truly original idea, you must free your imagination, challenge orthodoxy, and envision that which is not. . . . To spur imagination, organizations may ask questions such as 'What if we no longer did what we do now?'"[2] If they are curious about new concepts and listen carefully, a chip designer might get great ideas from a software developer, and a software developer might get tips from a chip designer. This is true across many engineering disciplines.

That very same mechanism that makes curiosity a powerful driver of innovation, makes it a powerful driver of inclusivity. It allows people to get past their preconceived notions of the value some colleagues bring to the table.

Every one of us has unconscious biases, and we often connect with people who look and think like us. We also reach out to the familiar when selecting leaders for key positions or brainstorming new ideas, even when we believe we are making objective decisions based on merit. In a 2018 *Harvard Business Review* article, Lori Nishiura Mackenzie and Shelley J. Correll explain that "when hiring, evaluating, or promoting employees, we often measure people against our implicit assumptions of what talent looks like"—what they call our "hidden template of success." This template, not surprisingly, often looks a lot like us: people who went to the same schools as we did, who've had similar career trajectories and shared similar experiences and perspectives.[3]

Mackenzie and Correll's research found that managers can block this bias by "closely examining and broadening their definitions of success." In other words, by being curious. If we start from that place, we are more likely to challenge our template and recognize and value good ideas on the table—regardless of who brought them there.

When we are open, we approach others and their contributions with an inquisitive mind and without judgment. Curiosity breaks down barriers between people, helps them build stronger relationships, and makes everyone feel valued and included. But it needs to be intentionally cultivated.

Engage in Continuous Learning

Mike Schroepfer, former CTO at Meta, was driven to work in computer science in Silicon Valley, where new ideas and innovation is the fabric of most startups, by a deep desire to learn. "[I] was driven by a curiosity to learn," he told me. "I felt that there was a bunch of people there I could learn from and ideas that would stretch me and allow me to grow." Curiosity is often regarded as the fuel for learning, as it was for Schroepfer. We learn to satisfy it; it drives our desire to find answers and try new solutions.

But our curiosity also expands the more we learn, because our understanding of a topic increases, leading to more questions. The more we learn, the more we realize what we *don't* know and how much more there is to discover. We see the interconnectedness of ideas, many of which we don't understand yet, and it sparks a desire to fill that gap in our knowledge.

As we explored earlier, when organizations get into the bad habit of rewarding people for doing things "how we've always done them" and working in narrow silos, employees' curiosity tends to wane (if it's not actively discouraged). To foster a culture of curiosity, encouraging your team to engage in continuous learning is critical.

Darby Dunn, vice president of production at Commonwealth Fusion Systems, told me that, as she and the founders of the clean energy startup were growing their organization, they wanted to create a culture where there is an eagerness to learn. "Something that I've emphasized a lot with my team is always look to absorb new information, learn more about the scientific aspect of things," she told me. This learning leads to "trying to figure out how to innovate, improve, and learn new strategies." For a startup that relies on developing breakthrough technologies for its survival, emphasizing an eagerness to learn nurtures the culture of curiosity it needs to succeed.

Encouraging continuous learning is critical in a fast-changing industry like tech. New tools, programming languages, frameworks, and methodologies emerge constantly, and keeping up-to-date with these developments ensures that your employees and your company can stay competitive. But for your organization to be successful, learning should not be limited to technical skills.

Hector Ruiz, the former CEO of AMD, took over from the organization's founder, Jerry Sanders, in 2002. "I strongly encouraged curiosity in my staff," he told me. Not everyone seemed to share that curiosity, though. At the time, an employee who was responsible for AMD's group in China did not exhibit the curiosity to learn and understand how the local needs differed from those he'd experienced in US sales. He wanted to run the China business from California, something that Ruiz observed was not going well—it suggested the employee was not interested in developing the knowledge of Chinese culture that would help him broker deep relationships with business leaders there. Hector decided to put in charge a Chinese American woman who was knowledgeable about Chinese culture and willing to move to the country. The Chinese computer company Lenovo, which had done zero business with AMD, soon became one of its largest customers there.

FROM THE SURVEY

"Attending seminars and collaborating with other organizations helped in developing and broadening my knowledge in applications of engineering and technology."

—**Black man, machine design engineer**

"My corporation has strong values in continuous learning and development, and I have completed hundreds of hours of training in just a few years."

—**Latina, computer systems analyst**

"Talk to people in the groups that need representation, and ask them what they need to be successful."

—**Nonbinary person, web designer**

"The CEO of Lenovo, who later became a good friend of mine, told me one day at dinner, 'Hector, the main reason I'm doing business with you is the decision to put a Chinese person in charge,'" Ruiz explained to me. He understood the value that this person—someone who not only looked like the target clients but, more importantly, also deeply understood them and was eager to learn more about them—would bring to the job. During his tenure, Ruiz promoted several people of color to vice president positions. But as he said, "It wasn't [promoting] diversity for diversity's sake." Their backgrounds combined with their unique perspectives led them to be curious in ways that were invaluable assets to AMD.

Collaborate with Others Across the Organization

One of the most effective ways in which a culture of curiosity drives innovation is by breaking down the silos that often show up between different groups. When technical staff become siloed, it tends to affect not only the flow of information but also the mindset of your staff. When ideas are not shared throughout the organization, teams and departments are not incentivized to explore outside their narrow focus. Employees are exposed to fewer new ideas, skills, perspectives, and knowledge from other teams or departments, stifling their curiosity over time. The more they "own" their narrow focus, the more entrenched their ways of doing things become, making them deeply resistant to change.

Encouraging your employees to work with groups in other functions—on either cross-functional or cross-cultural teams—helps to expose them to new ideas and ways of doing things to spark their curiosity and lead them to consider better ideas and collaboration.

Tzumu Lin joined VIA Technologies after graduating with a PhD from Caltech, where he and I were students together. He joined founders Cher Wang, a successful Taiwanese entrepreneur considered one of the top global women leaders, and Wen-chi Chen, who would serve as the CEO. Their company, first established in Fremont, California, initially made chip design tools to develop chips for the growing PC market. Eventually Tzumu, who was vice president of engineering, and his colleagues pivoted, deciding instead to make application-specific system logic that worked well with the processors of the day, such as those from Intel and AMD. They also established some of their operations in Taiwan and later extended into mainland China.

Over the next few years, VIA Technologies would acquire many companies in the United States to expand the scope of their business. Eventually Tzumu led engineering teams in California, Texas, Taiwan, and mainland China, all focused on developing innovative products. To keep a high level of innovation, all the sites had to work together, each taking a different part of the process. "One side may do the design, the other side will do the verification. They kind of cross-checked each other," he told me. Tzumu credits this global structure for the success of the company's innovation program.

He admits that bringing culturally diverse and global teams together is not always smooth. "There's a lot of tension. People always say, 'Hey, why do I need to work with different sites? Are they going to take over my job?'" The fact is that encouraging people from widely different backgrounds to interact is not easy; their unique perspectives will inevitably collide. If you are leading global teams, cultural norms will be radically different from location to location. There will be friction. And as humans, we want to avoid that.

Research from David Rock, Heidi Grant, and Jacqui Grey has found that while this friction is uncomfortable, it leads to better results. While homogenous teams feel easier, "easy" is bad for performance and innovation. "Research suggests that when people with different perspectives are brought together, people may seek to gloss over those differences in the interest of group harmony," the researchers write. But when we face the differences, we benefit from them.[4]

Creating a culture of curiosity—where people value others' perspectives instead of rejecting them—will lessen friction over time. When the various global engineering units at VIA Technologies started to see one another's value, they started working harmoniously and improved each other's positioning. "The two sites in Austin and San Diego worked closely with [the site in] Taiwan," Tzumu explained. "[Eventually they] didn't see them as a threat, but saw the value of helping them and actually offloading some of their work, but also helping them expand the market into different places."

Working closely with other teams and departments encourages your staff not only to find inspiration throughout the organization, but also to embrace the creative conflict that arises from differences.

Dig More Deeply into Problems

A culture of curiosity prompts leaders to see what others might have missed, to notice what's not there, to examine the data no matter how small, and to gain a deeper understanding of what is getting in the way of accomplishing their goals—whether creating a new product or helping every employee have an equal chance at success. If you want people to lead with curiosity, encourage them to dig into the root causes of the problems facing them.

Rebecca Parsons, the former CTO/CTO Emerita of tech consultancy Thoughtworks, once used a curiosity-led approach to prod the company's then-president to take action to increase diversity. In his monthly executive team presentation, the COO would show several slides, including one with the percentage of technical staff that were women. The numbers did not look good. "He would look at the slide, say, 'Oh well,' and move on. We did this three or four months in a row," she told me. "Finally, I had a call with the president. I said, 'You have two choices: You pull the slide out of the deck and admit you do not care about this. Or next month, when we look at the slide, we talk about what we might do to change it.'"

Challenging the president to move beyond complacency on this diversity problem and look more deeply into it sparked the executive team to become more curious about the lack of women in their tech ranks. When later in the year the executive team was selecting a group of candidates across the entire global operation for a leadership development program, they were able to see with more clarity the issues facing women in their company.

Each country was asked to put forward a number of potential candidates for the program. The criteria were that they were no more than three years away from being able to take over for the president, or at least be a direct report to him. "There were more lawyers and male lawyers than there were women in the entire group of nominees," Parsons said.

When they started to dig into the problem, the executive team realized they had not been looking at the leadership pipeline creatively enough. Instead, they were doing what they had always done. Based on their findings, this time they took a different approach to improving the numbers of women in tech leadership positions, a problem that had seemed hopelessly stalled months before. "We completely redid our global leadership development programs and went from just one program that was a feeder for [global leadership roles] to three programs," Parsons said. These different avenues allowed Thoughtworks to address the unique obstacles that were getting in the way of women advancing to leadership roles in their respective global regions.

The story illustrates how curiosity can be employed to overcome complacency around a known problem—and to solve it. Yes, it is good to look at the data, but what else is going on? And what will you do to change it? Every organization's solution may differ, and digging deeply into the problem allows you to try different solutions and learn from them. In the case of Thoughtworks, the company was global, so while the solutions for diversity and inclusion needed to be different in each region, the company's inclusion practices needed to embrace all the teams around the globe.

Digging deeply into a problem is particularly important in cultures where data is king. Data is often used in innovation to inform market response and reception to new product ideas. But when it comes to people problems, data usually doesn't tell us everything. Blake Irving, former CEO of internet domain registry GoDaddy, shared the story of how the company looked into compensation analysis to see if there was a salary gap between women and men. "We put up numbers to show how much women were being paid versus men. There wasn't that much discrepancy; it was pretty close. I'm looking at the data and thinking, 'This is not telling the story. There's something else happening here,'" Irving told me. "So we looked at promotion trajectory and [find] women have been in the same job two, three years longer than the guys and are making the same amount of money because they've been there so long."

Irving's curiosity led him and his team to see what others had missed. As a result, GoDaddy changed its promotion policy. For the first three years of their employment, regardless of whether they asked for it, everybody was reviewed for promotion. "We had a 35 percent increase in women's promotions," Irving proudly said. "Men's promotions didn't change."

Like Parsons and Irving, Bridget Frey, Redfin's CTO, saw a diversity problem within her organization and realized she had to investigate deeply to see it clearly and fix it. Curious about the root cause of these diversity problems, her team decided to approach them the way that they approached their software innovations. "We used JIRA, the same software we use to track bugs in our software. We made a list of all the problems we felt that we had around diversity and inclusion, and we prioritized them," she explained. "And then we started taking things off the list, just like we would do when we are building software for our customers. That approach identified several areas for us to start working on."

Frey's thorough and systematic mapping of the diversity issues allowed her and her team to gain a clear picture of what was going on. Asking deeper questions about the underlying cause of the issues helped resolve them one by one so that none could slip through the cracks or be forgotten. And it worked: a gender-diverse workforce became the norm at Redfin, and much of the diversity efforts evolved to increasing racial diversity, which Frey believes is still a work in progress.

Perhaps the most valuable benefit of habitually asking deep questions about the problems facing your employees is that it can help you uncover what's truly happening in the organization.

Caroline Simard, the former managing director at the VMware Women's Leadership Innovation Lab at Stanford, told me about companies the lab worked with whose leaders pushed back on looking at data by gender and race because the numbers were "too small"; instead, they grouped them together. This led her and two other researchers to write a piece in *Harvard Business Review* about the importance of looking at small numbers. "Pooling 'people of color' or 'women' to have more data discounts within-group differences and hinders meaningful change," they write. "An organization may be able to tell a clear story about how women in general are faring, or may be able to discuss the experiences of people of color broadly, but what about Asian women compared to Black women, or Hispanic men compared to white men?"[5]

Sadly, these companies' lack of desire to look deeper into what the data revealed is not uncommon. Many organizations ignore issues afflicting a small group of employees and focus on "the big picture." When they do, they fail to answer critical questions, such as: Are certain groups feeling more excluded than others? Why are we able to retain people from some groups but not others? Who is getting promoted or not—and why? What can we do differently to change this? Without digging deeper—with curiosity—into diversity issues, we cannot fix them.

For all of us, reintroducing our natural curiosity, asking questions, and digging into the root causes of problems can get us on the right track.

Challenge Assumptions of "How Things Are Done"

Perhaps nothing hinders the power of curiosity in an organization like hardened assumptions about how things ought to be done. These kinds of assumptions limit what we think is possible to what is familiar and already accepted. As a result, they often lead to incremental changes rather than significant improvements.

To boost your culture's innovation and inclusivity, encouraging your employees to question traditional approaches and solutions is essential. When we break free from them, we are able to explore new possibilities and uncover approaches that take the needs of *all* employees into account and allow them to contribute their best ideas.

Vijay Anand, executive vice president, R&D, at Apree Health and former CTO of Intuit, told me that his original lack of curiosity led him to make assumptions about the gender makeup of his staff that were not accurate at all. When a female tech executive asked him how many women he thought worked at Intuit India and how many they had hired, he admitted he had no idea. He assumed it would be half. "That's what I'm always used to, where there's plenty of diversity in the teams that I work with," he told me. "But then I realized that wasn't true. [The executive] pointed out the reality that at [my] executive table [she was] the only woman. If you looked at our overall engineering staff, about seven percent were women."

Anand realized that he had completely missed the point. His division, Intuit India, was doing a lot of work and growing fast, so he had not noticed this clear discrepancy in the staff. "When I then went in to go look at it deeply—Who are the seven percent? How did they feel?—[I] began my learning journey around how difficult it is to hire and retain technical women." Once he uncovered the issue, questioning his assumptions led him to understand the severity of the diversity problem in his tech organization and how to address it.

Nowhere is the power of challenging our thinking more evident than in the recruiting process. Reframing "success" and "potential" can prevent us from dismissing those who don't meet our entrenched, preconceived biases around talent. When we are curious to truly understand what people bring to the table, we will likely increase the pool of candidates and recognize talent where we might not have looked for it before.

Some leading companies get thousands of applicants, so they've developed efficient ways to target the most compelling candidates. Because these approaches have worked for some groups in the past, they become entrenched and are assumed to be effective ways to attract *all* talent. But often they have baked-in biases that keep the company from attracting the diverse pool of candidates needed to sustain creativity in the long term.

One of the ways companies have sorted through candidates in the past is by asking them to answer computer science trivia or solve a problem to demonstrate their technology acumen. The problem? Often these trivia questions or problems are unrelated to the skills that candidates would need to perform the job they are applying for.

Alan Eustace, former senior vice president of engineering at Google, said that questioning this approach and the assumptions underlying it was important for increasing the number of women that the company hired while he worked there. "If you have a small number [of women candidates], the last thing on earth you want to do is use 'weeder questions,'" he told me. "I can't tell you how many women we rejected because they didn't know some obscure piece of computer science trivia." Instead, he figured, when you have a smaller pool of candidates, a better approach is to do the opposite of weeding out: take the time to be curious and get to know their skills better. "Normally, we don't do reference checks for undergraduates, but [with] small numbers of people, we can afford to do reference checks. Before you reject somebody, why don't you actually call and talk to their adviser?" Eustace asked. "Or if it's a coin flip on whether you bring them back for another round, why don't you just give them the benefit of the doubt and bring them in for the extra round? Why don't you just do an interview that's aimed at whatever you're worried about? The idea is just to try to spend a little more time. I'm not trying to [lower] any bars. I'm just going to get the false negatives reduced to zero."

Like Google, many other companies have found time after time that while women often do not perform as well on weeder questions about trivia or puzzles, when hired as interns, where their skills have a chance to shine, they perform exceptionally well. For people of color this is even more true—there are so woefully few of them in most tech companies that weeder questions like the ones

Eustace described have an even great impact. Challenging the assumption that the approach reveals anyone's hidden potential is critical.

When recruiting candidates, asking questions that allow you to get to know the people in front of you and to understand their journeys can help you uncover skills and traits that add significant value to a product team. Considering all that a person brings to the table is not about lowering the bar of the technical skills required to do a job. It's about rethinking the skills that tech organizations need and about what talent looks like and where to find it, particularly early in someone's career.

Brianna Fugate, who we met in chapter 4, learned about Black Girls Code as a student in New York. The mission of the famed nonprofit strongly resonated with her. "I loved what they were teaching young girls," she explained. "I love that they gave them the confidence to like technology and build it." Fugate first started volunteering for the organization but then became interested in coding. Based on the team's recommendation, she applied for a scholarship to Google's Computer Science Summer Institute. The program selected a few students to travel across the country to learn from Google engineers. "In my mind, I had failed the interview," she confessed. "But I ended up getting asked to attend. I was one of the thirty students to go to Mountain View. It changed my life. And that ultimately is what led me to change my major from biology to computer science." She graduated with a computer science degree from Spelman College in 2018.

Fugate did not have the traditional profile that other candidates might have had—she certainly didn't fit the mold of what a great tech candidate might look like. But her story reveals that besides excellent technical skills, she brought other characteristics to her jobs: grit and guts. Fugate's ability to follow her curiosity and instincts—to try something so completely different from the major she had originally chosen, and to eventually change direction—shows her experimental nature, and the courage to scrap an idea and start all over if that's what the situation requires. If we don't similarly become curious about all skills that help technical staff succeed, excellent candidates like her will be ignored and organizations will miss out on high-potential talent.

Ana Pinczuk, who we met in chapter 2, found that her team at Anaplan needed to challenge assumptions about where talent could be found. She introduced the idea of recruiting hubs to attract candidates from a broader geographic area and a more diverse pool. "One of the hubs is in Atlanta where our data showed the opportunity to attract African American candidates," she told me. "Another hub is Austin, which has a large population of Latino candidates. We also attract great candidates at San José State, a large public university. We've been hiring a diverse population in Ottawa as well, including Canadian Indigenous people."

Bridget Frey and her team at Redfin have also turned traditional approaches to finding tech talent on their head. "I sat down with my team and we discussed innovative ways to recruit," she told me. They figured out that boot camps, for example, tend to attract a more diverse range of candidates than their more traditional recruiting sources. "I could get someone coming out of Harvard, or I could get someone from a boot camp program," she explained. So her team came up with a plan. Managers could open a position six months earlier than it was budgeted for. If they filled it with someone from a boot camp program, then they got to hire that engineer right away. "We had some people who were into that because they saw an advantage for them," she said. "These managers thought, 'If I find someone good, that's great. If I do not find someone good, I will not hire them.' And that is one way that we have been able to start diversifying."

Redfin's experiment has worked. When Amanda Zimmermann graduated with an associate degree in database administration from Bellevue College, she set out to look for a job with skills that were very marketable. All the major tech companies immediately rejected her, and it was clear that their automatic recruiting front-end systems had excluded her because she didn't have a bachelor's degree. So she decided that instead of searching for specific roles, she would search for unique tech employers.

"That's when I found Redfin. Redfin had a really extensive nontraditional hiring program. And they talked a lot about their values," she told me. It's recruiting approach made it clear that candidates from all walks of life could contribute to the company's goals. "They didn't seem like the kind of company that was just going to use me up and throw me away when they were done with me. They seemed like the kind of company where they were interested in investing in their people and growing talent from the inside." She secured a role at Redfin as an inventory software specialist.

Another example of Redfin's success is its participation with the Ada Developers Academy. Ada combines a six-month class-room experience and a six-month internship. Shari Meggs was a student placed at Redfin for an internship, and midway through, the company told her it would make her a full-time offer. "At Red-fin, I loved coming to work," Meggs told me. "I was learning some-thing every single day."

Kevin Scott, CTO of Microsoft, has also challenged traditional methods, which were inadvertently limiting the software giant's pool of candidates. "A normal hiring process is looking for reasons to say no to candidates," he revealed. Instead, he embraces finding talent in apprenticeship programs, much like the one that Meggs attended. "For these apprenticeship programs, we are looking for reasons to say yes. So, you are prospecting for potential," Scott explained. "You bring them in, and you are putting them through a structured apprenticeship program where they get on-the-job training, and they get a salary. At the end of six months, they have had this training, and they've had a chance to do at least one significant project, and you decide whether or not you convert them to full-time employees." Scott reports that the rate of converting program participants to full-time employees has been high.

Asking where you can find a broad pool of candidates like Brianna Fugate, what skills your team needs or your current workforce is missing, what hubs you can establish to consistently find underrepresented talent, and what talent actually looks like can all help you create an inclusive culture. And it all starts with pushing back on hardened assumptions about where talent can come from.

As you embark on nurturing a culture of curiosity, encourage your team to follow the examples of Eustace, Pinczuk, Frey, and Scott—and rethink your standard approaches to solving problems. Your curiosity about what is possible can guide how you develop products and technology as well as the processes that build an inclusive culture.

Curiosity Is a Human Endeavor

Erica Lockheimer, the former vice president of engineering at LinkedIn who we met in chapter 3, applied a natural curiosity to all that she did—and tried to inject that same sense of curiosity into the organization's culture. She regularly surveyed the staff landscape, looking for opportunities to promote more women. She would also tap people on the shoulder, letting them know, "I think you could do this. What do you think? I will support you." She would invite senior leaders for a fireside chat with the CEO, vice presidents, or talent acquisition staff to answer many of the questions she herself had. She founded LinkedIn's Women in Tech, an employee-led program that advocates for women in technical roles within the company. After leaving LinkedIn, she applied that same curiosity to found HumanizeHer, a platform aimed at featuring women's voices.

Fostering a culture of curiosity, like Lockheimer did, may seem simple in some ways. After all, we are born curious. Babies and toddlers constantly explore the objects and people around them, trying to make sense of the world. Even as they grow older, kids' insatiable openness leads them to ask "Why?" at every turn, to acquire new skills more quickly than adults, and to experiment and push boundaries. Encouraging people to ask questions and be open to new perspectives can help reintroduce curiosity into a culture that might have lost the sense of it.

But it won't be easy, and it will take time.

Breaking habits is hard to do. People like to stick to what is familiar and comfortable, to do what has proven to work before—even if a better but unproven alternative might exist. They don't want to risk failure or judgment. They want to play it safe. Yet despite its difficulties, building a culture of curiosity is a worthwhile effort for any tech company. Without it, innovation cannot thrive and opportunities are missed.

At the beginning of the chapter, I told you how hard it had become for students attending the Grace Hopper Celebration to meet the companies they most wanted to work for. Leading organizations were prescreening their candidates according to an inflexible set of criteria—one that often mirrored the criteria they used to recruit candidates outside the conference.

After looking more closely into the problem, we also found, though, that smaller companies didn't have the luxury to play this game. Unable to match the salaries and perks the larger companies offered, they couldn't compete for this small, elite pool of candidates. So, they looked broadly. Led by curiosity, they recruited exceptional talent that others had missed and attracted people who brought with them much-needed new perspectives and life experiences. They scooped up the talent that larger companies left on the table.

Sticking with the familiar, with what you already know, doesn't lead to breakthrough innovations. You shouldn't expect it to lead to a great change in your organization's diversity and inclusivity either.

ACTIONS

To create a culture of curiosity, encourage your employees to ask questions and regularly acknowledge those who offer new perspectives.

Engage in Continuous Learning

Encourage your team to explore ideas and learn new topics. Promote curiosity-fueled exploration in team meetings. Ask your team what topics and fields they want to learn more about.

Present talks and education. Focus on areas that are of high value to the organization. Record these talks so they are available to everyone.

Collaborate with Others Across the Organization

Share information and ideas between groups regularly. Find ways to introduce ideas outside your employees' comfort zones, including hosting speakers from other disciplines and from other groups at your company.

Create organizational-wide task forces. Bring together teams from throughout the organization to solve problems.

If you are global, ensure that you are encouraging your global teams to work together. Talk about ideas that came from across the organization.

Encourage your team to be open-minded. Show employees you are receptive to ideas from other groups or departments by inviting them and actively seeking them. Help them embrace the creative conflict that comes from collaboration.

Dig More Deeply into Problems

Encourage people to get to the root cause of a problem. Prompt them to ask questions that lead to a deeper understanding of a situation or challenge before acting.

Question the story painted by organizational data. Develop a practice for pushing back on the narratives that emerge when interpreting your data. Consider what the numbers are *not* telling you and whether you are interpreting them too broadly.

Challenge Assumptions of "How Things Are Done"

Rethink what is possible. Regularly evaluate the success of your processes and consider alternatives. Consider whether your approaches serve all needs, meet all objectives, or work only for certain populations or types of problems. Be suspicious of traditional methods that are considered sacrosanct.

Question traditional views of success. Reevaluate your organization's preconceived notions of what talent and high potentials look like. Consider which traits and behaviors that you look for in employees might exclude talent from certain groups.

‹6›
COMMUNICATION

Everybody needs to learn how to explain their work
to anybody. It's important, and it's amazing how few
people understand [that].

—Mary Lou Jepsen, founder and CEO, Openwater

A s a technologist, I've always known that articulating my vision and ideas is crucial to my success, although achieving it wasn't always easy.

At Actel, I became fascinated by the idea of using logic synthesis to let our customers map their designs to our field-programmable gate array products. This was a new idea at the time, and I was eager to pitch it to the executives. I was given ten minutes to talk with John East, the company CEO, and his management team. I didn't often present ideas to him; in fact, I was inexperienced at giving business presentations in general.

I spent a lot of time preparing the pitch, and when the day came, I gave it my all. At the end of my presentation, you could hear the silence in the room. Then John said words that I will never forget: "I don't get it." My expertise was at the intersection of software (how our customers used our devices) and hardware (where we developed and programmed our FPGA products). But most of the senior executives in the room, including John, came from the chip world. I did not translate my technical idea into language that made sense to executives from that background.

John asked a few questions, and several other people made a few comments. In the end, he approved the investment but made it clear that he arrived at this decision because he believed in me rather than because I had communicated effectively. Certainly, one of my lessons that day was that I needed to develop better communication skills in presenting technical ideas to leadership.

A technical team's ability to talk about their ideas—and listen to those of others—is vital to the success of product innovation. I've learned through experience that creating a culture that encourages open communication and candid discussion directly affects your organization's results. It isn't just about speaking up or using the correct language, although both are important. It's about listening, exchanging knowledge, and respectfully disagreeing or having difficult conversations. To create a culture of open communication, you must:

- Allow everyone to voice their ideas

- Provide all employees opportunities to develop their technical presentation skills

- Listen—to everyone, everywhere, all the time

- Deliver clear, bias-free feedback

- Learn to communicate across cultures

- Manage challenging conversations with compassion

Communication underpins many other aspects of an innovation culture. When you demonstrate courage, it is by speaking up. When you demonstrate confidence, it is by thoughtfully choosing with your words and actions. When you demonstrate curiosity, it is by asking questions. Open communication is the key to a culture where innovation and inclusivity thrive.

Allow Everyone to Voice Their Ideas

When it comes to communication, the culture at many tech organizations is problematic. Engineers are socialized to speak loudly and over others. The myth of the lone genius, explored earlier in the book, has much to do with this behavior.[1] In a tech culture that reveres individuals whose brilliance is perceived as solely responsible for innovations—rather than collaboration and the cumulative efforts of many—they become de facto role models. It's no wonder that team members in such cultures feel compelled to communicate in ways that primarily elevate themselves and their ideas rather than contributing to open dialogue, the exchange of ideas, and collaboration.

Emma Catlin, an engineer with a computer science degree from Brown, worked at Pinterest for several years after graduating but had difficulty being heard when she started her career. "I was having many problems with some coworkers talking over me in meetings," she told me. "Some of them just have very powerful voices, and my voice cannot compete. I have a softer voice, so I physically can't talk over them when they start talking." Although Catlin moved past it, the experience made a significant part of her time at Pinterest unnecessarily difficult.

However, the person who speaks the loudest and the most does not necessarily have the best ideas. Listening only to the loudest people means you will likely continue to get the same perspectives again and again.

Unconscious bias also plays a role in which voices are elevated in tech organizations. Deeply held stereotypes of the value team members from marginalized groups bring are often manifested through microaggressions: they are interrupted or spoken over when they try to contribute in meetings, their ideas are devalued or dismissed unless supported by dominant voices, and their perspectives are not considered seriously. Younger or less experienced employees can have similar experiences.

Shanna-Shaye Forbes, an embedded software engineer with a master's degree in computer science and an electrical engineering degree from UC Berkeley, recalls making a suggestion during a meeting and being ignored by her manager. The manager, however, responded positively when another team member, Brian, brought it up again. "Brian was much more senior. So my manager didn't hear my idea when I said it, but when Brian parroted it, he heard it," she told me. Looking back, Forbes wishes that she had been louder and had repeated her suggestion. But it was her manager's responsibility to make sure she was heard too. Leaders must be aware of their unconscious bias and how it leads to disadvantaging some groups in the workplace—and develop strategies to avoid these problem areas.

In my survey, which was gender-balanced in responses, 79 percent of men and 69 percent of women indicated that they felt heard and valued. For women who fall in the intersection of two underrepresented groups, the numbers are even lower: 66 percent of those with disabilities, 63 percent of Indigenous women, and 60 percent of Black women reported that they were heard and valued.

I have served on several advisory boards at universities along with graduates who are now successful engineering executives. Because these members graduated ten to twenty years ago when there were few women studying computer science, I have sat on more than one board that is almost exclusively men. Out of twenty people at one advisory board meeting, there was only one other woman besides me, a successful entrepreneur and executive I'll call Lucy. The chair of the board and the head of the engineering department were engaged in an animated conversation about research. Some of the other participants were occasionally able to add to the discussion. Lucy attempted to ask a question once, was interrupted twice, and was talked over four times—and still could not get a sentence in. Finally, out of frustration, I demanded the chair give Lucy a chance to speak. I am not sure she appreciated my intervention. But as I witnessed the dynamic of the all-male exchange, I was uncomfortable with the culture it was communicating and had to speak up.

This experience was hardly unique. Research shows that men talk more than women in meetings—and women are interrupted far more often than men.[2] To create a culture of open communication, where the Emmas, Shannas, and Lucys of the world have a chance to be heard, leaders need to interrupt the interrupters, call out behavior that diminishes the quality of open exchanges, and ensure that everyone can speak.

Mike Schroepfer, the CTO of Meta for many years, offered me his perspective on this issue: "If you want to counteract many of the built-in barriers [women and members of underrepresented groups encounter], you have to intervene and ensure they speak up, contribute their ideas, and feel heard." Schroepfer understands that leaders cannot take a passive role in this task. The best tech executives find ways to prevent the same extremely vocal participants from dominating every discussion, and they call on every meeting attendee when necessary.

Hector Ruiz, the former CEO of AMD, was one of those executives who would call on people. "Nine out of ten times when I've called on somebody quiet in a corner of a room, and I said, 'Hey, you've been listening for one hour to the discussion. You must have an opinion. What is it?' What comes out of their mouth is amazing," he told me. "I think that's something [we] can do more of . . . because it is too easy to ignore their participation."

"I wished I had an advocate in the room with me to keep my colleagues accountable for their tone, ensuring they were acting and speaking respectfully. Being the only female engineer has been difficult for me, not from experiencing big, overt sexual harassment but from the mountain of microaggressions and small items of disrespect."

—White woman, electrical engineer

"One of the companies [I worked for] . . . had an open weekly meeting that fostered people being heard."

—Asian woman, CTO

"[The] executive level of my current company is really supportive. There are open and safe discussions about gender stereotypes in tech, why they exist, and what can be done to remove them. Having these led by men, in a male-majority team, is extremely useful to create a culture of equality and mutual respect. Having high-level execs like the CEO, vice president of engineering, and CTO not just respect their female employees but truly value their contribution to the company makes for a very neutral, nurturing, and safe environment."

—Asian woman, software engineer

In the early days of AnitaB.org, we tried to ensure that everyone had a chance to share their ideas by using a communication style called the Thinking Environment, developed by Nancy Kline, author of *Time to Think: Listening to Ignite the Human Mind*. In this model, every person in a meeting is required to speak for a few minutes. After everyone has taken a turn, there is an opportunity to speak again. Although at times this approach made an interactive conversation challenging, the technique ensured that all voices were heard and often led to meaningful discussions. Some organizations use a modified version of the Thinking Environment when hashing out new ideas.

Innovation is a team sport. The quiet engineer and the loud, boisterous one may, working together, find the breakthrough that can change the company's future. Creating a culture where everyone has a chance to contribute and be heard allows innovation and inclusivity to thrive.

Provide All Employees Opportunities to Develop Their Technical Presentation Skills

For technical workers, learning to talk about their ideas is critical.

I first discovered the importance of communication in graduate school at Caltech, working with an extraordinary visionary, Ivan Sutherland, often considered the father of computer graphics. A month after I arrived, Ivan told me that I was to present our research on how to exploit hierarchy in large-scale chip designs at a biannual corporate meeting. I still remember that presentation. I sputtered through the ideas still in development and lingered on unimportant details. I shook the entire time I was speaking. But I did it, and I was grateful to Ivan for the opportunity.

Afterward, he took me aside and gave me feedback on how I could improve. But he also congratulated me. Only later did I fully realize the gift that Ivan had given me just two months into my graduate career. All the corporate attendees now knew who I was—the only woman presenting that day—and, more importantly, what my work was about. They didn't just notice a young female graduate student; through my stammering presentation, they learned about the importance of what Ivan and I were exploring. This experience was one of the first times I grasped that talking about ideas is as important as developing them.

Al Zollar, former CEO of IBM Lotus Software and member of the NASDAQ board of directors, had a similar moment when he realized the value of building trust with customers, including overcoming perceived racial bias. He told me about a presentation he made to one of his first accounts that turned into a major early-career milestone. Throughout his presentation, the senior customer executive, a white male Southerner, was quiet even though his staff members in attendance seemed quite engaged. Later, his boss told him the customer wanted him removed from the account. Zollar was shocked. He knew the presentation had been well received by the staff, so he didn't quite understand what had gone wrong. Zollar had a haunting suspicion that race was a factor. His boss believed in him, however, so she convinced the client to keep him on for a trial period and supported him by assigning a senior systems engineer as his mentor. When this engineer listened to Zollar present, he offered him clear advice: "That was a really great presentation, but you use the word 'I' way too much. Your job is to make *your* idea the *customer's* idea." That insight made all the difference to Zollar in future interactions with customers. Ninety days later, the same Southern-born senior executive told Zollar's boss, "Never take Al off my account."

Every researcher and engineer eventually learns the lesson that being able to communicate their technical ideas effectively is key to moving up the ladder. Many hone their skills by presenting at conferences, product reviews, or all-hands meetings. These experiences offer invaluable opportunities to talk in front of a broad audience that may not yet be familiar with the topic. That's why leaders must expose as many of their team members as possible to technical presentations—both delivering and attending them.

Another place where individuals can develop their communication skills is internal forums. These play an important role in technical organizations, exposing young employees to the best ideas and products and getting them excited about the future. The format of internal forums varies, but ensuring that the best ideas are being presented and there are speakers and participants with diverse perspectives and from different parts of the organizations is critical. Done well, they can signal to the entire engineering workforce that the company enlists contributions from everyone.

Nick Donofrio, the former IBM executive we met in chapter 3, designed and led a technical forum at the company every year. "These forums are opportunities for us to assess ourselves and be openly critical of ourselves, and to appraise and evaluate ourselves," he told me. "I made it all about business, about making IBM better. But in the process, if we can feature extraordinary people from diverse backgrounds, this helps the company." Marie Wieck, a former general manager at IBM, told me that "in addition to recognizing technical experts, [Nick] really tried to make sure that there were speakers that celebrated our diversity. . . . For example, if there were three people that could present on an invention and one of them happened to be African American, they might be chosen to present, or a woman or someone with a disability."

Being deliberate about featuring employees who are one of a few—who are women, Black, Latine, Asian, or LGBTQ+, or who have a disability—not only helps them develop technical communication skills but can significantly impact your entire culture. Having these team members speak at technical forums and meetings signals to everyone that you value their contributions and normalizes the concept that great ideas can come from anyone.

Some larger companies host internal technical forums explicitly targeting underrepresented groups. Kim Warren-Martin, a longtime engineer at Intel who eventually worked on women's programs, told me that Intel's Women Principal Engineers Forum made a difference to many women engineers. "There was a goal to get more women on the business side, and in technical ranks to the top," she said. "The principal engineers forum for women was set up to bring all of them together from around the world. Included in the forum [were] mentors who could talk about the principal engineer track." I spoke at one of the first meetings of the group and observed the experience of many women in the room. They took pride in sharing their technical ideas even though many were deeply uncomfortable being singled out. Many attendees from those early forums went on to successful technical careers at Intel.

Most tech companies, though, are not large enough to host their own technical forums. That's why encouraging your employees to attend similar events outside your organization is essential. The Grace Hopper Celebration, as well as gatherings such as the Tapia conference and those hosted by the Society of Hispanic Professional Engineers and AfroTech, have grown in popularity precisely because companies have increasingly supported their technical staff in attending, especially after seeing how these conferences positively impacted them. More recently, I've noticed some companies select their top engineering executives to attend these conferences and then offer their employees get-togethers on location, providing opportunities for unstructured conversations between engineers and their leaders. On several occasions, young engineers who attended such intimate discussions at the Grace Hopper conference sought out leaders from their companies who were also attending—often someone from a different division with whom they didn't normally interact—and pitched them an idea. In one instance I am aware of, a social media researcher had great ideas about adding features to an existing product, which eventually were adopted by their company.

Diane Greene, former CEO of VMware, told me about a an internal technical forum she hosted at the company. "We had an internal engineering conference [once a year]. We would rent out some large space and solicit papers," she told me. "The engineers would write proposals. And the principal engineers would review [them] and select the top ones for presentation at the conference. Everybody else would be part of a poster session. We would also have a two-day conference that all the engineers, including QA, would attend. They highly valued the offsite and it was very fruitful."

Listen—to Everyone, Everywhere, All the Time

Ensuring all team members can share their ideas, receive feedback in productive and respectful ways, and get exposure to technical presentations are all important ways to create a communication culture. But fundamental to these efforts is the act of listening. Listening means not just hearing what someone says but also understanding their intentions and what they convey with body language. It requires genuine empathy for and interest in the other person—so when we listen intentionally and sincerely, we can build trust. And when there's trust, you have stronger relationships, learn from each other, and collaborate better.

Trust is different from psychological safety, which I discuss in chapter 2. According to Amy Gallo, author of *Getting Along*, psychological safety is "a shared belief held by members of a team."[3] But trust is about one-on-one relationships. Employees experience trust when they believe their managers and leaders respect them, are acting fairly and in good faith, have their best interests in mind, and keep promises.[4]

Michael C. Bush, CEO of Great Place to Work, says that listening is the most important thing you can do to develop trust with your employees. "True listening requires humility, vulnerability, and empathy," he writes. "You may have lots of opinions, but to be a for-all, inclusive leader, you must put those opinions aside. If you are having a conversation and you are not willing to consider other points of view, what's the point of having a conversation at all?"[5] Trust and listening are intertwined, creating a virtuous cycle.

That's why it's critical that at every point in your organization's processes, you ensure that your staff hear one another, not just mark time until the other person finishes while thinking about their response. To create a culture of communication, above all, you must hear feedback from your employees, particularly those who might feel isolated due to being an only.

There are many ways to create space for employees to share their experiences and concerns—and be heard. Affinity groups or employee resource groups (ERGs) are one of the most effective ones when set up properly. (I will discuss ERGs in detail in the next chapter.) These groups create a safe place for employees to open up about the obstacles they face when contributing their ideas and collaborating with others. They can be an important lens for understanding your organization, so creating opportunities to listen to members of these groups and their feedback should be a top priority. Over the years, I've seen the success of ERGs in tech organizations be directly tied to how closely leadership takes their feedback.

Darby Dunn, formerly a senior leader at SpaceX who, with a few other women, founded the company's Women's Network, believes that much of the reason the ERG succeeded in creating positive change was because its sponsor, Gwynne Shotwell, the president and chief operating officer, listened to their feedback. "One topic that came up was specific demeaning or derogatory phrases that [members of the network] had heard in meetings or on the shop floor—and we never wanted to hear these phrases ever again," Dunn recalled. "I took that list [of phrases] and presented it to Gwynne. Within an hour, she sent out a companywide email telling employees not to use these words again. Although the email did not guarantee that these phrases would never be used again, it signaled to the entire organization that words matter. The opportunity for members of the ERGs to surface feedback during a private meeting [with] the president clearly made a huge difference."

Another powerful way to create space to listen to employees' experiences is through stay interviews. Sabina Nawaz, a longtime executive coach and leadership adviser, explains that the key to stay interviews "is asking questions that address what you'd learn from exit interviews."[6] Ask employees—well before they have a chance to quit—if they feel that they're valued, their contributions are recognized, and there is a path toward meeting their professional goals. Ask if their talents are being maximized in their teams, if there are tasks or challenges they wish they could tackle, or if there are skills they want to develop. Ask if they feel they are able to speak up—and be heard—in meetings, and if their work or the culture causes stress. And, above all, ask if they feel like coming into work every Monday. If they do, what would it take to maintain those feelings for many years to come? If not, what can you do to improve their experiences and how can you support them better?[7]

Because burnout among people of underrepresented groups in tech is so common, you must have these conversations early and frequently. "Fold [these questions] into your existing one-on-one meetings with your employees, or if you don't have regular one-on-one meetings, consider conducting stay interviews monthly," Nawaz recommends.[8]

Stay interviews are impactful because asking your employees from underrepresented groups about their experiences communicates that you care about their needs and value their contributions. In particular, having a conversation about their future and listening to any issues they are having sets a path for them to stay. When a company is downsizing or experiencing tough times, Colin Parris, CTO of GE Digital, believes stay interviews are more important than ever. "People are going to be recruited right away, especially when your business is falling," he told me. That's when recruiters sweep in. That's when you need to ask your team members, "What's *your* dream?" Once you listen to them, then you can show them how you can create a path for them to succeed, explained Parris. "I'll give you experiences. I'll put you in rotating programs. I'll give you mentorships. You will meet people from the outside to build your network. . . . I have a four- to five-year plan for you."

Other structured spaces you can create include listening sessions where leaders make themselves available to meet with employees for an open dialogue about what's going on in the organization, or in response to a traumatic world event or crisis, especially one that disproportionately affects members of an underrepresented group. These meetings often have to be put together quickly—but it should be done thoughtfully. Ask and listen to the employees most affected about the most helpful way to design and hold the session.

I learned that lesson the hard way. In 2014, feeling that men had to be part of the solution to the problem of too few women in tech, I had this naive idea that we should include a plenary panel of men at the Grace Hopper conference. The men I asked to be on the panel believed in and were committed to creating a culture of innovation that welcomed women, and we wanted to highlight the importance of male allies. The panel included Alan Eustace, Mike Schroepfer, and Blake Irving—executive leaders featured in this book—and Tayloe Stansbury, at the time CTO of Intuit.

It was an unmitigated disaster.

These four men were earnest in their desire to help create a different future for their organizations. But I had not anticipated the anger many attendees would feel about men taking center stage in a conference meant to highlight women. Before the panel began, an ad hoc group distributed bingo cards to attendees that included stereotypical sentences or comments men frequently use to discuss women in their organizations, their support for inclusion initiatives, or why there are not many women in their companies.[9] These included, "Calls a woman articulate," "My mother taught me to respect women," "That would never happen in my company," "Blames 'awkward geeks' for abusive behavior in tech," and "Asserts other man's heart is in the right place."[10] Occasionally, an audience member called out "bingo" during the talk.

Although the panel failed—and I take full responsibility—what happened next was also remarkable. The men on the panel quietly arranged for a room they could use the next day for a listening session. Eustace, Schroepfer, and Irving posted on social media, reaching out to those who were most vocal about the lack of credibility of the male allies panel to ask them to join the new session. At the hourlong meeting, the panelists just listened. They didn't speak. Women, many of whom worked at their organizations, spoke up fearlessly about the many issues they had encountered, including how some people in their HR departments had papered over their concerns.

It was a brutal session. And I applaud the courage of the women who spoke their truth and the panelists' courage in listening to their feedback. Eustace and Schroepfer told me that the session forever changed their understanding of what women go through in tech organizations. They returned to their companies and started addressing the most egregious bad behavior, including identifying problem employees.

Remember that listening in an unstructured, casual way can be powerful too. If your organization does not have formal spaces where people can share their experiences, you must take every opportunity to listen to them. Drop by their desks and ask your team members how they are doing and how you can help them do their jobs more effectively. And ensure all employees of underrepresented groups have someone who will listen to them—even if what they have to say is uncomfortable—and support them. Aicha Evans, former Intel executive and CEO of Zoox, told me about a time when she had participated in a "tense debate about a topic" at work. She left the debate upset about how she was treated. So she called one of her sponsors, Stacy, for advice. He listened to her and then gave her advice on how the situation could be handled.

Evans was able to trust her sponsor's advice because she felt heard by him. When people don't feel heard, however, trust breaks down. They don't believe you'll do much to support them or stand by their side.

Deliver Clear, Bias-Free Feedback

The value of having a culture of open communication is put to the test most vigorously when leaders must provide feedback to employees. Evaluating performance and helping people grow is one of the sacred responsibilities of leadership. In the past, annual performance reviews were the standard followed by almost every company I know. Today organizations provide feedback much more frequently. Many tech companies conduct shorter, twice-a-year performance reviews, and others have ditched the annual or bi-annual review for spontaneous or monthly feedback. Regardless of the frequency, to create a culture of communication, you need to regularly help employees understand how they're doing.

And yet, most of us need more guidance on giving feedback. Sometimes we rely only on the recent evidence of an individual's performance, rather than looking at the arc of their entire history. All too often, we can fall prey to several other cognitive biases as well. The *halo effect,* for example, leads us to give more positive feedback to people who are well-liked or known to be good performers in certain areas.[11] The *horn effect* does the opposite: it leads us to give negative feedback to someone across various dimensions because of one mistake.[12] *Confirmation bias* causes us to find evidence of either poor or positive performance—depending on our preconceived notions of someone's capabilities.[13] When you add these cognitive biases to the fact that underrepresented groups are often the target of unconscious biases, stereotypes, and double standards, it's no surprise that women in my survey report receiving vague or little feedback, hampering their chances to improve, grow, and succeed.

A Black project engineer survey respondent reported that she stayed in the same position for seven years, with the promise of a promotion dangling over her. "[I received a] lack of detailed feedback during performance evaluation sessions [and] few concrete details on how to improve unless I pushed for the answer," she wrote.

Other women also had issues with evaluations. "I was consistently gaslighted on my performance," an Asian software tech lead reported. "The worst experience I had was with a project I worked hard on and released. It resulted in a double-digit increase in business metrics. My manager/tech lead got a promotion for that project, but I was given a 'meet expectations' rating. When I asked about it, I was told the initial release had a bug. This is when I decided to leave the company."

In other instances, employees from underrepresented groups receive negative feedback that would be viewed positively when applied to a white male team member. "As a very outspoken female engineer and an emerging leader, I've been faced with the 'likability' bias throughout my career," a white survey respondent wrote. "While people know that I am capable of producing great results and executing large tasks, I often receive quite a bit of feedback about being too 'assertive,' too 'ambitious,' etc." Being assertive and ambitious is typically seen as a leadership quality in a man.

Research confirms that women and people of color are short-changed when it comes to feedback. For example, women are more likely than men to receive inflated, overly nice feedback that doesn't help them advance.[14] They are less likely than men to receive constructive comments that they can use to improve performance.[15] And they are more likely to be given feedback on their personality traits rather than on performance.[16] Black employees, meanwhile, are more likely to be scrutinized and receive lower performance reviews.[17]

Françoise Brougher, the former chief operating officer of Pinterest, told me how these biases affect women's careers, including hers. "Men—it's all about potential. Women—it's what they have done," she told me. "There is [also] a stereotype of women, [that] she's either too motherly and not tough enough, or she is just so aggressive [that she] cannot work with colleagues. I was accused of both in my career. I was told I was probably right in the middle. I think there is all this bias and stereotype that you find in performance reviews and everywhere else; [they are] just major obstacles of you being able to move forward."

To create a culture of open communication, leaders must give meaningful feedback that is free of bias to *all* employees—

members of underrepresented groups as well as those of the majority, and from entry-level employees to senior engineers—so they can perform at their best. The art of delivering feedback is outside this book's scope, but there are three critical actions that every leader can do to improve:

1. **Don't wait for the annual review to provide feedback.** A lot happens in a year. Unless you are taking detailed notes to keep track of someone's performance, you'll likely fall prey to recency bias and focus your performance on the most recent task, achievement, or misstep—and ignore what happened before then.

2. **Focus on performance, performance, performance.** "Where we find the bigger biases are in evaluations of people's personalities, their future potential, and on the mentions of exceptionalism," researcher Shelley Correll said in an interview.[18] Focus on what is quantifiable—the results and work that an individual has accomplished.

3. **Provide clear, concrete, and actionable feedback.** Be respectful and compassionate, but don't avoid being candid out of fear of hurting your employees' feelings. Constructive feedback requires that you provide concrete advice on how employees can address any performance-related issues—and specifics on what they can do to up their game and advance in the organization.

What's most important for leaders to understand is that the quality of the feedback they give significantly impacts their ability to get the most out of all of their employees, retain their best talent, *and* meet their innovation goals. Being thoughtful about how you deliver it and mastering the art of it is worth the time and effort.

Learn to Communicate Across Cultures

Technology companies are global by nature. Most of the large tech companies, like Apple, Google, Cisco, Applied Materials, and more, employ thousands of employees in technical roles around the world. Many managers lead teams of engineers, software developers, and technology staff spread across multiple countries and cultures. For too many people, communicating effectively in these culturally diverse teams is about overcoming language barriers, but overcoming cultural barriers is often more impactful. Creating productive, collaborative, and innovative environments that are also inclusive and fair requires cultural awareness and adapting to a range of communication styles and norms.

People from different cultures have different ways of expressing themselves, interpreting information, and interacting with others, particularly with authority figures. For example, in many Western cultures individuals expect to voice their opinions openly and directly, even to superiors. However, in countries like India, Japan, or South Korea, communication may be more indirect, with an emphasis on avoiding confrontation and being respectful to those with power. All too often, rather than being aware of and working to understand these differences, managers make biased assumptions about their employees based on their communication styles. They might think employees from cultures where communication is more indirect lack confidence or leadership presence, when in fact, the opposite might be true.

A culture of communication focused on building trust across these divides requires deliberate effort. You need to invest time in learning about your team members and showing respect for their customs, values, and traditions. You also need to be particularly mindful of understanding how their cultural norms might differ by gender.

Geetha Kannan is one of the pioneers in leading efforts to increase the number of women in tech in India. She grew up professionally and eventually ran HR at Infosys, an IT consultancy firm that was instrumental in helping India become a global destination for software services. Today she is the founder and CEO of Wequity for Women and Technology, an Indian organization dedicated to maximize the potential of women and the organizations that employ them. Kannan said that positive changes are happening in India when it comes to societal expectations of women, but progress is still gradual. While they are increasingly recognized for their contributions, traditional views still emphasize putting others first.

"It's so ingrained that women are responsible for the home, so you are not put on the best projects ever," she told me. "There is often a concern among managers about the potential for women to take marriage leave or relocate due to their husband's job." Kannan noted that Indian managers, wanting to be considerate, sometimes limit work assignments for women, unintentionally hindering their growth and advancement. These societal expectations also make it difficult for women to display the kinds of traits that Western companies in particular associate with success and leadership potential. Kannan shared the story of a woman who came up to her after an event, crying. "She said, 'I'm supposed to be a very docile kind of creature at home, then you come here and tell me be bold.' So she was asking me, 'How do I transform myself? How can I be one person at home and one person at [work]?'"

Being aware of how cultural expectations impact people of different groups in your global organization can help you break stereotypes, ensure equal opportunities for everyone, and support and retain talent better. To learn more about your employees'

cultures and to help overcome language barriers, prioritize regular face-to-face meetings over communicating solely via email
or messaging platforms. Videoconferencing helps you notice tone
and body language, while written communication, particularly
short-form methods, can lead to missing nuances. Most important, managers should provide plenty of opportunities for team
members to share aspects of their culture during these meetings.
Nurturing curiosity can lead to mutual understanding and respect. And when we respect others we welcome their ideas, collaborate better, and innovate better—all while creating an inclusive
environment.

Manage Challenging Conversations
with Compassion

We all falter at some point—you'll make a misstep, your employees
will make mistakes, and your company will struggle, too. Having
difficult conversations is unavoidable.

"If you build an environment that is based on trust . . . your staff
[will] grow to know that you are either going to tell them the truth
or you're going to tell them that you can't tell," Bob Nunn, the former CEO of Everactive, explained to me. "This gives them a comfort that they're not going to be left out in the dark." When he was
the CEO of a startup, he heard others express how hard it was to
be blindsided with bad news about the company's performance.
They told him, "We were kept in the dark, and then all of a sudden
the news was bad and everyone was in trouble." Since then, during
difficult times "we've been open," he told me. "We've been telling
people not to freak out, that we will tell them what is coming."

As hard as many of these conversations are to orchestrate, if
you don't have them, great people leave because they don't see a

path forward. Today, however, many tech leaders are finding some of the toughest conversations they have are on the topics of DEI and politics (both domestic and international). In fact, the more open your communication and the freer people feel to speak up, the more likely that difficult conversations will surface.

Brianna Fugate, a Black software engineer we met earlier in the book, told me that immediately after George Floyd's murder at the hands of a Minneapolis police officer in 2020, the event was weighing heavily on her mind and heart. She was fearful for herself, her family, and her community. "This one coworker decided to say something, and it was a little tone-deaf to the situation," she told me. "It was something along the lines of, 'We should be grateful that we even have jobs, and we should just try to push all the negative out.'" Fugate was upset and enraged. "I wrote in Slack something like, 'I'm going to log off for the evening. I just want to say this week was hard. It's as hard for everyone else as it was for me. Take the time to rest and to be at peace. Some of us, unfortunately, can't *not* focus on the things that are happening in the world. We don't have the privilege to be able to ignore what is happening.'"

When Fugate came to the office the next day, she had a meeting with senior leadership. Her manager up the hierarchy had seen the message and took the time to talk to her. "He's a white man, and he said, 'You know, I'm very proud of you for standing up for yourself,'" she told me.

Fugate found the strength to speak up. But equally important, leadership listened and supported her. Providing safe spaces for sensitive information to be spoken and heard is critical to navigating difficult conversations.

"[Intel] had the courage to sometimes moderate and facilitate very difficult conversations amongst people from different backgrounds," Aicha Evans, CEO of Zoox and former Intel executive, told me. It also made employees feel safe when reporting or communicating sensitive feedback to the company. "[Intel] instituted a hotline, an anonymous place to go if you had an issue. It was originally intended for people who are not in the majority, but it was open to people who are in the majority," Evans explained. "People could call up that line and say, 'I feel like I'm being isolated or excluded,' or 'I don't think this is fair.' Or 'my manager is not inclusive,' and so on and so forth. I think that soft stuff actually ended up being way more important because you're signaling your intent to do something about this." I've heard many Intel executives discuss this hotline and provide examples of changes the organization made based on feedback that was given anonymously through it.

Communication is an essential skill for organizational culture. Words matter, and how you label ideas matters. The best organizations find ways to have difficult conversations and support people who speak up and speak their truth. I encourage you to reflect on your organization and how you support speaking up, especially for those who are one of a few.

ACTIONS

To create a culture of communication, make it the underpinning of every aspect of how the your tech organization operates, encouraging all to speak and ensuring that all are heard.

Allow Everyone to Voice Their Ideas

Actively manage participation in meetings and key discussions. Ensure everyone has an opportunity to share their opinion by seeking out input from every person in the meeting, directing specific questions to or drawing out those who have not yet contributed.

Prevent the same people from dominating key discussions. Set ground rules for every meeting that emphasize respect even as they allow for people to disagree. Redirect the conversation when only the same few people are talking. If some members of the group are consistently shut out, consider the role unconscious bias might be playing. Intervene when people talk over each other, and call out when someone repeats a colleague's suggestion without giving them credit.

Provide All Employees Opportunities to Develop Their Technical Presentation Skills

Create informal exchanges between leaders and technical staff. Establish forums or listening sessions where employees and leaders can interact to discuss technical ideas.

Offer wide access to technical talks. Ensure there is a broadly diverse set of people presenting ideas to your leadership team and to the company overall. Consider sending employees to external events so they can both be exposed to technical forums and practice participating in them if there aren't any opportunities in your company.

Listen—to Everyone, Everywhere, All the Time

Make listening an explicit goal. Model it to your team by listening intently to employees in meetings and discussions. Show empathy and humility; don't just kill time until the other person finishes. Remind people that listening is more than half the job of communicating.

Create safe spaces for employees to share feedback. Support employee resource groups and solicit and listen to their feedback. Conduct regular "stay interviews" with members of your team to talk about their futures and their needs.

Deliver Clear, Bias-Free Feedback

Review your processes. Encourage managers to provide feedback regularly. Train them to avoid cognitive biases—such as the halo effect, the horn effect, and confirmation bias—by basing performance on transparent and clear standards. Provide concrete and actionable feedback to *every* employee.

Review your reviewers. Assess the process for delivering feedback, and make changes to ensure it is fair and consistent, emphasizing performance over personality. Evaluate managers for how clear, concrete, and actionable the reviews they deliver to employees are.

Learn to Communicate Across Cultures

Educate yourself on cultural differences on your team. Meet with site leads from all locations and learn more about the cultural backgrounds of the team. Use this knowledge to design inclusive communication norms, and train others to do the same.

Develop trust across cultures. Meet regularly with site leadership to understand common communication challenges and evolve processes accordingly.

Manage Challenging Conversations with Compassion

Engage in difficult communication with respect and curiosity. Don't shy away from tough discussions, and hold managers accountable for not shying away from them either.

Acknowledge and support team members who surface difficult conversations. When an individual raises an issue, point out that it took courage to speak up, and listen with empathy. Ensure that the conversation is resolved in a manner that is effective.

‹7›
COMMUNITY

Building a community that celebrates, supports, and
empowers differences is the solution for everyone.

**—Jennifer Chayes, former managing director, Microsoft
Research; dean, College of Computing, Data Science, and
Society, UC Berkeley**

W hen I first moved to Silicon Valley, I worked at a research lab in Palo Alto. While the idea of technology
changing the world had captured me, I arrived with
a deep yearning for community. I had loved being a graduate student at Caltech, but I was also very much aware of being an *only*.
I longed for a community of women who shared my passion for
technology. But the research lab was small and there were not
many women. Fortunately, my boss introduced me to his wife,
Amy Lansky, who had recently graduated with a PhD in computer
science from Stanford University.

The computer science department at Stanford had a strong
women's organization at the time. Through Amy's introduction,
I attended a panel it hosted featuring women technical leaders.
Led by another Amy—Amy Pearl—who was also a recent graduate
from the program, the panel included Barbara Liskov from MIT,

who ultimately received the prestigious Turing Award; Susan Owicki, a Stanford professor; and Barbara Simons, a researcher at IBM and future president of the Association for Computing Machinery. It was extraordinary and fed my soul. After the panel, I joined some of these women for dinner. For a young woman starving for community, that evening was magic. It changed my life forever. It reminded me that I was not alone and inspired me to reach for what was possible.

Later that year, my boss invited me to his and Amy's annual Halloween party, which was attended by technologists from around Silicon Valley. These parties were legendary—I still meet people who remember them! It was there that I met Anita Borg, fully decked out in a Halloween costume. We developed a strong connection and became close friends. We discussed how to create a women's community and hosted dinners with other women in technology. While we worked in tech, most of us doing research, our conversations often turned to making a difference in the world.

Many of the women I met in those early days remain my friends today, although most of them have long since left technology. As I navigated my career, they advised me and discussed my most challenging dilemmas and decisions. Years later, when Anita and I founded the Grace Hopper Celebration, they were very involved. When my relationship with a man whom I had expected to marry collapsed, resurfacing grief from a greater loss—the death of my mother when I was fifteen years old—they were there to help me. It was a difficult time. This community of women—and Anita in particular—provided a place where I could fall apart and, ultimately, move forward constructively in my personal life *and* career.

While writing this book, I interviewed forty-six people in depth, and over the course of my career, I've talked to tens of thousands of engineers and computer scientists. One theme that kept coming up in all of these conversations was community—the desire for it and its importance to individuals. Community is the glue that holds us together and provides nurturing, tough feedback and support. And it has a direct impact on innovation.

To develop high-impact technology, you and your employees must take risks and contribute ideas so the best ones can surface. And to do that, as we explored in the previous chapters, people need to feel safe and accepted. Community provides this safe place. People come together when they have a common goal, vision, or identity. Community is the structure that encourages belonging. In fact, community and belonging are interrelated and complementary; I often think of them as the soil that allows individuals to sprout, grow, and become vibrant flowers. You need both.

When you feel like you belong in a community, you are willing to step out of your comfort zone and take calculated risks. You question how things have been done in the past and share your ideas because you're not afraid of being ridiculed or waved away. When you feel like you belong, you feel connected to others. You trust them and their capabilities. You form good working relationships and collaborate far more effectively. And the very aspects of community and belonging that support a culture of innovation also foster inclusivity.

To create a culture where community thrives, you must:

- Communicate that you value everyone with your actions

- Provide opportunities for your technical teams to connect and bond

- Create safe spaces for members of underrepresented groups

- Encourage employees to find community outside the organization

A culture that strives to value everyone, to accept them for the unique perspectives that they offer, is more likely to retain talent. That diversity of thought and experiences, in turn, brings a broad set of ideas into the mix, fueling innovation. Community is the foundation of that virtuous cycle. The other five Cs in this book— creativity, courage, confidence, curiosity, and communication— will not take hold if you don't have community. Every member of your technical staff, regardless of their role, needs to believe that the work they are doing matters, that they are part of something bigger, and that they are respected. If they do, they will deliver much better results for you and the organization.

The Importance of Community and Belonging

Community is an important part of all our lives. Humans feel a need to find people they trust and can confide in. "Belonging is essential to humans," write DEI consultants Julia Taylor Kennedy and Pooja Jain-Link. "Psychologists rank our need to belong on par with our need for love."[1] Belonging is just as important in the workplace, where the boundaries between professional and personal lives often blur. Evidence, for example, shows workers stay in a job longer when they have friends.[2]

That need for belonging is even more deeply felt by people who are isolated because they frequently find themselves to be an only in their department, division, or team. Many feel pressured to leave their authentic, full selves at home. In their workplaces, the frequent microaggressions and stereotypes they experience or witness signal that they don't belong, but also pressure them into conforming to narrow expectations of success. Women, for example, might keep their femininity or emotions in check as they might be seen as counter to the "standard" of successful performers—a standard, of course, based on men. People of color may feel like they must code-switch or downplay their cultural identities to fit in. And so on.

Shanna-Shaye Forbes, a senior software engineer, told me that earlier in her career, she felt that she didn't belong on the team she was assigned to at a big tech company. She was one of the few women and Black people, and one of the youngest members on her team. "Before I quit, every Sunday I would go into a funk: 'Oh, I have to go back [to work] again. I have to go back.' . . . I asked to [move] to another team, and my manager said, 'Yeah, that's not happening anytime soon.' . . . I don't think he wanted me to leave his team. But I knew I couldn't stay." Unfortunately, according to my survey results Forbes's experience was not unique. While 68 percent of men reported a sense of belonging at their organizations, only 53 percent of women, 52 percent of Blacks and Latines, 50 percent of Black women and Latinas, and 41 percent of women with disabilities felt the same. There are many people like Forbes who leave a job because it isn't working for them. They perceive that something isn't quite right, that they don't fit in or are not able to be themselves.

Not being able to show up authentically affects individuals' well-being and undermines innovation and the organization's overall success. When people downplay parts of who they are to fit in—or at least not to stand out any more than they already do— they become disconnected and alienated from others. Their stress increases, and their morale decreases. It is exhausting. Over time, this disengagement leads many to leave the organization. This is one of the reasons so many women quit the field. According to data from consulting firm Accenture, half of women going into tech drop out by age 35.[3] "If you lack a sense of belonging, it can be very difficult to envision yourself having a long career at a company or inside of a team," explained Kevin Scott, CTO of Microsoft.

Building a culture of community starts with committing to accept and value all employees and welcoming them to show up authentically in your organization. It also requires creating opportunities for people to connect and bond with each other; supporting safe spaces—smaller, more intimate communities where individuals can connect with others like them—especially for underrepresented groups; and encouraging employees to find communities that feed their souls outside of your organization as well.

Communicate That You Value Everyone with Your Actions

Leaders set the tone for how the organization views and treats people. Building a strong community starts with you. Your job is to let employees know that they belong, that they have a place in the organization, and that their contributions matter—regardless of who they are. If you are a member of the dominant group in your company, communicating that belonging is possible for all is that much more important.

Over the years, I've met many well-meaning leaders committed to developing world-class products who say they support diversity and inclusion. But they hold these two goals as separate. Time after time, they articulate their support of inclusion, but when they approach important technical efforts, they reach out to the people they are most comfortable with, mostly white or Asian men. They often, consciously or unconsciously, place talented members of underrepresented groups in a distinct box and treat them with kid gloves. They don't give them the opportunities and hard feedback they provide other employees. So, while they say they support inclusion, their actions say otherwise.[4]

And their employees—those they unconsciously exclude, like Forbes in her early job experience—hear them loud and clear: *You don't really belong here.*

To signal that every member of your team is accepted for who they are, you must do it with words and actions alike. Mike Schroepfer went beyond mere words when he instituted a training program for allies at Meta. "[We] focused on trying to activate people who look like me to get more involved in helping people [who don't] day-to-day in the company," he told me. "What I hear from people all the time is that the small problems add up over time. So, things that sound inconsequential to people who don't suffer [really matter]. [They] have their work get credited to someone else, they get interrupted, they do not get invited to the right meeting." With this training program, Schroepfer sought to help other leaders understand the many ways in which microaggressions diminish some employees' sense of belonging and offer them ways to intervene positively and restore the feeling of trust and community.

Even communicating to employees that you value everyone's opinions goes a long way toward encouraging a sense of belonging. When that is a value that's promoted relentlessly, it can become part of a company's north star. Bob Nunn and his leadership team at Everactive thought deeply about how to articulate the importance of diverse perspectives. "We really like ... talking about the value of bringing different viewpoints to the table," he told me. "And I think that helped a lot."

How you show up and whom you put in charge also communicates a sense of belonging more clearly than words. Al Zollar has served on six public boards, including at NASDAQ. At two of these companies he was the only Black director, but he still felt welcome. "The two companies where I was the only Black person on the board had really great cultures," he told me. "I think they had tried to have more Blacks and people of color on their boards

"Working with a team that's made up of BIPOC [Black, Indigenous, and people of color] women made me realize that engineers shouldn't compete but, instead, should know how to cooperate and use their strengths together."

—Latina, software engineer

"I wish I had realized the importance of community when I first started; it's like compound interest. I'm involved in a pilot mentoring program sponsored by our Women in STEM employee resource group. It's been a great experience. We are learning and growing and inspiring each other. It gives me an opportunity to share some of the things I learned the hard way."

—Black woman, electrical engineer

"Companies should embrace and promote . . . community engagement. Today, with meetups and other social forums, there are much more powerful, more organic tools available. And many are free."

—White man, data scientist

but had not been as successful as they wanted to be." So, what made him feel like he belonged despite being the only one? One of these companies, Red Hat, had an incredible culture around open source and inclusiveness. "Jim Whitehurst, who was their CEO at the time, once showed up at a companywide all-hands meetings wearing the T-shirt of the Red Hat Black affinity group," Zollar explained. "That was a statement."

When someone joins your organization—or even your board—you have a unique opportunity to communicate they are welcome from day one. The most obvious way is by ensuring you have a deep, diverse bench of executives, which signals to employees that everyone has a chance to succeed in your organization..

During my time at AnitaB.org, IBM was well-known for going above and beyond in making Black employees feel like they belonged as soon as they joined. From day one, new hires would be assigned a Black executive mentor who made sure their doors were always open for any issues that new employees might encounter. I respect and admire the processes that companies like IBM create to make their employees from marginalized groups feel like they belong.

I often wish that some of today's high-tech companies that have become household names—and which are well meaning and earnest in their desire to create cultures that are diverse—would learn from legacy companies about how to create community. All too frequently, organizations reinvent diversity and inclusion programs (usually expensively) but fail at the most important task: helping everyone feel that they belong. Without community, diversity and inclusion programs don't have the impact they should.

Provide Opportunities for Connecting and Bonding

"Folks tend to have a greater sense of belonging if they have a cohort of work friends, people they feel like they can be their authentic selves and feel social connection with," Kevin Scott told me. Friends make the workplace more enjoyable and fulfilling. They share their victories and vent their frustrations. They provide career and emotional support when things get challenging.

Friendships help the long hours at work feel more meaningful—and make them go faster. When employees feel connected to each other on a personal level, they are more engaged and loyal to the organization. Friendships help to reduce stress, boost morale, and foster trust and collaboration. They're the salve that organizations need to create community and a sense of belonging.

Friendships are grassroots, though; they almost always grow organically. And while you can't control that, it is in your best interest to provide opportunities for them to develop and blossom. At the startups where I worked, we often got together for fun, be it a lunch, a birthday party, or a milestone celebration. These kinds of social events can sometimes feel forced, but they are a good way to help employees make connections.

Diane Greene held scavenger hunts every year at VMware to help employees develop connections throughout the company. "We would run really difficult hunts on the Stanford campus," she said. "I carefully assembled groups of five to seven people in which no two people were in the same function in the company. We'd have a finance person, a sales person, an engineer, a support person, and so on. And it would take two to three hours to complete. Those proved to be phenomenal because once people got through them, they knew someone in every function in the company whom they were comfortable calling about anything. I always heard from people after I left VMware about how they enjoyed working with one another and collaborating on the success of the company." Approaches like the one that she employed can create a sense of ownership and community throughout her organization, but they also reinforce a culture of creativity.

Today, when so many employees work remotely, it's even more important to bring the team together in person at least a few times a year to nurture that sense of community and belonging. At AnitaB.org, we gathered all our staff, including those based in

India, once a year. The connections formed in person made our virtual meetings more effective because team members developed relationships. If it's not possible to bring the whole team together, then make sure employees have opportunities to meet virtually for purely social reasons—such as a videoconference lunch meeting or coffee break. Just make sure it's during work hours so everyone can participate. You can also dedicate an hour a week for remote team members to log in to a videoconference where everyone works independently and silently but at the same time, so they still feel like they are working "together." Not only does this create a sense of community for remote workers, but it also allows for serendipitous collaboration. If someone is struggling with a task or wants to consult with others, they can do so. Many companies also use communication software such as Slack or Teams to have ongoing technical and social conversations.

Create Safe Spaces for Underrepresented Groups

To create a culture of community, you must establish intimate, safe spaces for underrepresented groups where they are encouraged to speak freely and learn from each other. Many, if not all, of the technology companies I've worked with over the years have created such spaces—either affinity groups or employee resource groups (ERGs). And when appropriately supported (and funded), the best of them are incredible assets to the organization.

Many people from underrepresented groups—including female, LGBTQ+, Black, Latine, and Indigenous employees, for example—attend their first ERG meeting in search of community. When Darby Dunn launched the LGBTQ+ ERG at SpaceX, she wasn't at all sure how many people would attend. She was positively

surprised when a substantial number showed up at the first meeting, almost all in search of community. "[The ERG] was a way for
folks to know that they weren't alone," she told me. "They might
be the only LGBTQ+ person on their team, but there's actually
somebody else who sits five rows down. Because unlike gender
and racial identity, mostly you can't tell [who's LGBTQ+]."

ERGs are also spaces where those in underrepresented groups
can share experiences and express their frustrations without
having to code-switch, fit in, or face harsh judgment. In other
words, they offer a sense of belonging and validation. Knowing
that there are other people like them, who understand what they
are going through, can be affirming for employees who often feel
isolated.

Above all, ERGs can offer community and emotional support,
helping employees digest and cope with traumatic societal events.
For example, in the United States during the Covid-19 pandemic
Black people died at the hands of white police officers, violence
toward Asian people increased, and gay people were targeted in
mass shootings. After such events, ERGs helped employees come
together, engage in open dialogue, and process their feelings
about these events, leaning on each other for support. Knowing
that they are not alone and that others share their concerns can
help employees encourage and learn from each other.

In addition, ERGs can offer programming, including networking and professional development activities. They can provide
opportunities to interact with and become visible to senior executives, too. Among their many benefits, these activities boost
feelings of belonging by showing members of underrepresented
groups that they are valued in the organization.

Not all ERGs and affinity groups are created equal. I once
gave a talk to a new women's group at a well-known tech company. Its members wanted to make a difference but, as a whole,

felt powerless. Management instructed them to meet only during lunchtime to ensure the group did not detract from their work hours. They were given no budget, and their leaders were volunteers. This is a classic example of an affinity group created simply to check a box in the DEI to-do list. Launching one without proper support does not communicate to the entire company that you are interested in what members have to say or in their bringing their authentic selves to the organization. A common and ineffective outcome of such a ERG group is that it becomes a coffee club where participants chat and share their discontents. These complaint sessions scare away many members who are interested in solutions and often defeat the original purpose of ERGs. In other words, they create the opposite of a culture of belonging.

Effective ERGs and affinity groups need to receive support from leadership, a budget and program help. Dunn helped to create two ERGs at SpaceX: a women's network and the LGBTQ+ group. She believes the key to their success in creating a strong community for their members was the support of the president of SpaceX, who not only approved both groups' creation but also carefully listened to their feedback. Dunn was encouraged.

Sarah Loos, a senior software engineer, was similarly encouraged by the response she received from leadership when she and other women at Google, where she used to work, created an informal network of women in the research group. "It started with social lunches once a month, and then it snowballed into more programming," she explained to me. "But you need admin support. You need somebody to make the calendar events, to send out the reminder emails, to make the reservations, to do all of this stuff. [The company leadership] ended up giving us some percentage of time of a program manager, who then helped us do more events and more planning. And that took off a lot of the load and also made it much more scalable."

Support from top leadership is critical for ERGs and affinity groups to become effective tools in fostering community. Blake Irving was committed to creating an inclusive culture at Go-Daddy. Among the many practices he embraced as CEO was establishing affinity groups. "We started the GoDaddy Women in Tech group," he told me proudly, "and I started recruiting speakers." He invited me to be among the first speakers, and I was impressed with his commitment. Beyond funding the program, he and his executive team regularly listened to the feedback from the group. At the time, GoDaddy's reputation had suffered significantly from a series of Super Bowl ads featuring scantily clad women. But it was clear that Irving was determined to change the company's culture. It is hard to overstate the impact he made, and how dramatically one senior leader can shift (over time) an organization's core values to create a sense of community where everyone feels welcome.

To be successful, ERGs must also be nimble enough to meet the needs of their members. As diversity and inclusion have received more attention in recent years, many ERGs have been formed in larger companies and are managed by HR and DEI departments. While HR might establish and enforce rules for these groups with the best of intentions, their rules can often squelch the community rather than encourage it. I have spoken at a number of women's conferences that were officially sponsored by women's ERGs that included tens of thousands of members. When such groups host gatherings, they can provide access to role models from a range of backgrounds or conduct meaningful surveys for their members. But they can also struggle to provide intimate discussions and feedback for individuals. That is why, at large organizations, you might see division-specific ERGs, such as the one described by Loos, that offer a more focused and intimate sense of community; groups based on technical topics, such as research;

or location-based groups, such as local women's ERGs in various cities where the company is based.

ERGs are not the only way to create safe spaces in your organizations. Emma Catlin, who I introduced in chapter 6, is currently head of engineering at Formally, and before that was a software engineer at Pinterest. While at Pinterest, she had a standing get-together with six other women in the organization with whom she met every two weeks for lunch. "It was really nice to talk to other women who were in different organizations and different teams," she explained. "They knew what I was doing, but when I shared difficulties about some of my coworkers, they didn't know exactly the people I was talking about, which I considered a good thing."

Gaby Aguilera, a medical doctor and former software engineer in test whom I wrote about in the introduction, sometimes felt alone at Google, where she took her first job. As an immigrant from Mexico who arrived in the United States in high school, she often felt like she didn't belong at Google or in the field of computer science. That changed after she attended a conference where she became connected with several women who were spread throughout the giant company. "We would attend [each year] and get to know each other, and then we would come back and see each other and talk," she told me. Those connections gave her a sense of belonging and a community at Google that served her well during her time there.

Encourage your employees to form connections and community with other people within the organization, like Catlin and Aguilera did. Ask your employees if they would want to meet others who share similar experiences, and serve as matchmaker if you can—sign them up for professional development courses where they might meet employees like them, or, if you can, send them to conferences where a big contingency from your organization is attending.

Encourage Employees to Find
Community Outside the Organization

Not all companies have ERGs for their employees. Tech startups or medium-size companies in particular might not be able to support a large number of affinity groups. When these internal communities are either lacking or not robust enough, it's critical that you encourage employees who are at risk of not feeling like they belong to find a community outside the company, one where they can show up authentically and share their experiences with others like them.

As the cofounder of the Grace Hopper Celebration, I had a front-row seat to watch many women who joined the conference for the first time seeking that community their companies couldn't always provide. Women who attended from across the United States had the chance to connect with peers from other companies and other divisions at their company. Those connections often remained long after they left the conference.

Raquel Romano received her PhD from MIT. She was initially ambivalent about attending women-only events as she, like many women (including me), felt she should not need extra support simply for being a woman in a technical field. When she was exploring a job transition, someone in her leadership chain encouraged her to attend the Grace Hopper conference. "I remember Grace Hopper being transformational for me and thinking, *Why have I not done this since day one?* It was magical, It was not at all a place for women to complain or cry about our plights," she told me. "It was a place where it was eminently clear that what brought us together was our passion for our field, and that we were strong, independent, competent, perfectly capable women who also could gain strength from having a unique space for conversations."

Many smaller communities have surfaced to serve the specific needs of their audiences. In 2006 six Latinas bonded at the Grace Hopper conference and founded Latinas in Computing, a group by and for Latinas with the mission of promoting their representation and success in computing-related fields. They regularly held lunches at subsequent conferences and remained connected to their growing community the rest of the year, including nominating senior Latinas for prestigious awards. In the following years other communities were established, such as Black Women in Computing and a diverse set of international groups. Huma Hamid and Farah Ali, for example, created Pakistani Women in Computing, a community in both the United States and Pakistan that convenes regularly and virtually through events and podcasts. The Grace Hopper conference in India launched in 2010. All of these communities were created and led by members of the tech field to provide a safe space for like-minded professionals to communicate, ask tough questions, and celebrate their achievements.

Of course, there are other large, very successful organizations around the United States that celebrate their communities. Leanne Pittsford created the wildly successful Lesbians Who Tech for the LGBTQ+ community. More than fifteen thousand people attended its 2023 conference; the group obviously meets a critical need. Valerie Taylor and colleagues founded the Richard Tapia Celebration of Diversity in Computing Conference, and subsequently launched the Center for Minorities and People with Disabilities in Information Technology, which focuses on tech participation for Blacks, Native Americans, Indigenous people, Latines, and people with disabilities.

In addition to communities based on identity, people have created technical-focused groups such as Women in Cybersecurity, Black Women in AI, LatinX in AI, Women in Big Data, and Women in Data Science. Members of these communities provide support and advocacy, allowing members to strengthen their innovation muscles and learn to show creativity, courage, and confidence, as well as develop curiosity in their careers—in a safe space.

As a leader, communicating that you support your employees who want to find outside communities shows that you value them and their contributions, that you accept and acknowledge that they might need critical help that perhaps is not available in your organization, and that you are willing and committed to assist them in finding it. And when you tell someone, "Your need to belong is valid and I encourage you find it wherever makes most sense for you," you are telling them, "We support you because we want you to succeed, because you belong here." So help your employees expand their networks by providing opportunities for them to participate in events. Encourage them to network online in some of the communities I've listed above or to attend local or online meetups. And mentor them on how to connect with others via platforms like LinkedIn.

Communities for *All*

Leaders who have grown up professionally surrounded by others who look like them might not immediately understand the importance of community or a safe space where people can show up authentically. For white men, the familiarity of their environment can unconsciously reinforce their sense that they belong—and, as humans do, they often assume their experience is universal. As a result, many white men don't realize the extent to which groups such as women and people of color might not feel that same belonging. They might not relate to the isolation that their colleagues feel in places where there aren't others who look like them and whose experiences are similar to theirs. They might not be able to understand, for instance, the midcareer engineer who approached me at the Grace Hopper conference in 2017, sobbing. She worked at a large tech company and told me she wished she had learned sooner that this kind of community existed for her. She had never felt like she belonged in her workplaces.

For those who have been in the field for a long time or have been leading engineering teams for a while, it is likely you have established a community for yourselves—either in your organizations or outside. It is easy to forget the life-changing impact that communities can have on younger employees, whether they are members of underrepresented groups, recent grads who are living in a new city, young parents who are juggling work and family, or anyone else in need. Shanna-Shaye Forbes, for example, belonged to a young employee network when she joined HP as a software engineer. "We would get together after work for tapas or something like that," she told me. "It was really nice to meet new hires and younger employees, people similar to me in age." Employees hunger to connect with others who understand them and share their experiences at work.

Often, it takes seeing the positive impact that a sense of community has on another person to remember how much we ourselves depend on and benefit from it. Many of my board members at AnitaB.org were male engineering executives at large tech companies. After attending the Grace Hopper conference, several spoke to me about the transformation they saw in their female employees at the conference. The experience was transformative for them as well.

However, most managers aren't attuned to how much harder it is for members of underrepresented groups to find a community. These managers often shut down or don't support them when they request to attend conferences, local meetup events, or internal networking opportunities that might help them feel a sense of belonging but take place during work hours. At a student conference, a senior technical manager who was on one of the panels confided to me that her well-known tech company didn't support her participation. She participated on her own. Although she has a desire to mentor the next generation of women in tech— and proudly represented her organization (a powerful recruiting tool)—the message she received from her leadership was that it was not important.

Just as leaders focus on developing the technical skills of their staff, they need to also develop their employees' skills in fostering inclusivity so that seeking community outside the organization isn't the only option for members of underrepresented groups. Knowing how to create cultures of community and belonging should be a capability every manager is required to develop. Because when you provide opportunities for people to experience communities that feed their souls, you help them grow professionally and personally—and that in turns helps your company succeed. It helps you retain the technical talent you went through so much trouble to bring in, and by tapping into the connections they develop, it helps you attract new talent too.

Communities are places that help improve the experience of belonging for all individuals, and ultimately, it is your job as a leader to ensure that belonging is felt by *everyone*. Like nurturing all the other Cs, fostering community takes work and attention. But the payoff is worth the effort.

ACTIONS

To create a culture of community, provide spaces for your employees to come together and encourage them to join groups that align with their identities and interests, either inside the company or outside.

Communicate That You Value Everyone with Your Actions

Show all your employees that they belong. Actively promote the value of bringing diverse groups of people together in all-hands meetings and presentations. Prove that you value everyone's opinions and perspectives by acknowledging them and listening to them in discussions and meetings.

Ensure that your onboarding process is inclusive. Make sure that people joining have a mentor and know who to ask questions of.

Provide Opportunities for Connecting and Bonding

Bring your team together for celebrations and social events. Convene significant portions of your employees for celebrations or social meetups. Consider hosting programs like coding competitions or scavenger hunts during work hours to gather your employees together socially while contributing collectively to a project.

Gather everyone on a regular basis. Bring together international team members for strategy and team sessions. If that isn't possible, create virtual meetings with structured conversations.

Create Safe Spaces for Underrepresented Groups

Create locally led ERGs for underrepresented groups. Ensure that the ERGs have financial and administrative support. Support professional development programming and networking opportunities for group members.

Ensure there is a safe place for all your employees to share and make connections. Support and encourage people

to find community by hosting networking events in your
company. Regularly communicate your support of community groups.

Encourage Employees to Find Community Outside the Organization

Assess where the gaps are in community groups. Evaluate
the full breadth of the internal groups you offer and identify who isn't being served by them.

*Provide a budget and framework for participation in
outside conferences.* Financially support your employees
in attending outside events. If money is an issue, consider
setting aside a fixed number of conference registrations
with a process for individuals to apply. Support their participation in virtual conferences where community development is part of the content.

< CONCLUSION >

Diversity, inclusion, and belonging is the business
imperative of the future. If you don't get that, you lose.
—Colin Parris, senior vice president and CTO, GE Digital

I love technology and the opportunities it provides for our world. I can feel and see how some of the extraordinary inventions we hear about every day could positively impact our future long after I am not around to participate.

I see more women, people of color, LGBTQ+ people, and people with disabilities creating products that will change our lives, like Mary Lou Jepsen at Openwater, who is helping make the next generation of medical technology, and Fei-Fei Li, an AI researcher at Stanford and cofounder of AI4All, who is focused on the next generation of AI leadership. What is most encouraging to me is the changing mindsets of many leaders who are deeply committed to technology development *and* understand that inclusive cultures are deeply intertwined with innovation.

I am optimistic about our future, but change happens over time and takes patience and commitment. Years ago, I visited Nepal and trekked to Mount Everest's base camp. It was a twenty-day climb. Every day we increased our altitude by one thousand feet, ultimately reaching an altitude of eighteen thousand feet. It was a great model for achieving your goals—step by step.

I hope the tools, examples, and stories I shared with you in this book help you build a culture of innovation and inclusivity—one that is a positive force in the world. I truly believe that if you embrace the six Cs—creativity, courage, confidence, curiosity, communication, and community—you will find that your organization thrives.

But while writing this book, I've also learned more Cs that can support the cultures we need. *Collaboration*, for example, is the heart of creativity—and while it's supported by every one of the six Cs, in and of itself it carries much of the weight in an inclusive culture. And effective *change management* is also a critical C for large companies seeking to transform. If you want to create change at your organization, and you have a vision for what that will look like for technical innovation, then developing a change management process that supports inclusion is critical.

I worked in technology for twenty years and then served as CEO of AnitaB.org for another fifteen years. I've had the opportunity to work closely with almost all the technology companies whose products you use daily. I remember Google when it was a startup! I remember that in 2007 we invited technical executives from all the large tech companies that are household names today to attend the newly created Technical Executive Forum. I listened to the confidential conversations of these executives who were grappling with creating an inclusive culture. What I took away is that so many leaders want to create highly innovative, highly inclusive organizations. They want to do things differently than what has been done—and failed—in the past, but they're still figuring out what it means in their organization.

This book is because of all of them—and for all of them. My message is that things can be different. Embracing creativity, courage, confidence, curiosity, communication, and community can help change your organization—and your life as well. And it can help you change the world.

NOTES

Introduction

1. "Mead–Conway VLSI Chip Design Revolution," Wikipedia, https://en.wikipedia.org/wiki/Mead%E2%80%93Conway_VLSI_chip _design_revolution, accessed November 6, 2024.

2. Mary Harrison, "She++ Documentary on Women in CS Earns National Attention," *Stanford Daily*, March 4, 2013, https:// stanforddaily.com/2013/03/04/she-documentary-on-women-in-cs -earns-national-attention/.

3. Caroline Criado Perez, "The Deadly Truth About a World Built for Men—from Stab Vests to Car Crashes," *Guardian*, February 23, 2019, https://www.theguardian.com/lifeandstyle/2019/feb/23/truth -world-built-for-men-car-crashes.

4. Emily Olson, "'You Could Feel the Cutthroatness': Droves of Men Took over This Women's Tech Fair," NPR, October 6, 2023, https://www.npr.org/2023/10/05/1203845886/women-tech -conference-men-grace-hopper.

5. AnitaB.org, "Top Companies for Women Technologists: 2018 Key Findings and Insights," https://anitab.org/wp-content /uploads/2020/09/top-companies-insights-report-2018.pdf, accessed November 6, 2024.

6. AnitaB.org, "Top Companies for Women Technologists: 2022 Key Findings and Insights," https://anitab.org/wp-content /uploads/2022/12/AnitaB_2022_Design_Final-Digital_update.pdf, accessed November 6, 2024.

7. AnitaB.org, "Top Companies for Women Technologists: 2023 Key Findings and Insights," https://anitab.org/wp-content/uploads /2023/09/TCReport2023_Final_Web.pdf, accessed November 6, 2024.

8. Russell Contreras, "Anti-DEI Bills Targeting Colleges Have Surged Since 2021," Axios, January 31, 2024, https://www.axios .com/2024/01/31/anti-dei-bills-target-colleges-surge-antiracism;

Elizabeth Dwoskin, "How a Liberal Billionaire Became America's Leading Anti-DEI Crusader," *Washington Post*, February 10, 2024, https://www.washingtonpost.com/technology/2024/02/10/bill-ackman-end-dei-industry/.

9. Emily Peck, "The Israel-Hamas War Is Creating Tensions at Work," Axios, November 6, 2023, https://www.axios.com/2023/11/06/israel-hamas-war-workplace.

10. Jeff Nelson, "3 Reasons DEI Programs Fail," *Fast Company*, March 1, 2024, https://www.fastcompany.com/91044583/3-reasons-dei-programs-fail-and-how-you-can-prevent-it.

11. Ruchika T. Malhotra, "Do Your Diversity Efforts Reflect the Experiences of Women of Color?," hbr.org, July 1, 2019, https://hbr.org/2019/07/do-your-diversity-efforts-reflect-the-experiences-of-women-of-color.

Chapter 1

1. Justin Fox, "How Silicon Valley Became the Man," hbr.org, January 9, 2014, https://hbr.org/2014/01/how-silicon-valley-became-the-man.

2. "Don't Be Evil," Wikipedia, https://en.wikipedia.org/wiki/Don%27t_be_evil, accessed November 6, 2024.

3. Susan Fowler, "Reflecting on One Very, Very Strange Year at Uber," susanjfowler.com, February 19, 2017, https://www.susanjfowler.com/blog/2017/2/19/reflecting-on-one-very-strange-year-at-uber.

4. Erin Griffith, "Pinterest Settles Gender Discrimination Suit for $22.5 Million," *New York Times*, December 14, 2020, https://www.nytimes.com/2020/12/14/technology/pinterest-gender-discrimination-lawsuit.html.

5. Nitasha Tiku, "Google Hired Timnit Gebru to Be an Outspoken Critic of Unethical AI. Then She Was Fired for It," *Washington Post*, December 23, 2020, https://www.washingtonpost.com/technology/2020/12/23/google-timnit-gebru-ai-ethics/.

6. Chauncey Alcorn, "Google CEO and HBCU Leaders Discuss Talent Pipeline for Black Tech Workers," CNN, updated February 1, 2021, https://www.cnn.com/2021/01/31/business/google-hbcus/index.html.

7. AnitaB.org, "2023 Top Companies for Women Technologists," anitab.org, https://anitab.org/research-and-impact/top-companies/2023-results, accessed November 6, 2024.

8. C. Hovey, M. Beldon, S. Sundar, and W. DuBow, *NCWIT Scorecard: The Status of Women in Technology* (Boulder, CO: NCWIT, 2024).

9. Vivian Hunt et al., "Delivering Through Diversity," McKinsey & Company, January 18, 2018, https://www.mckinsey.com/capabilities /people-and-organizational-performance/our-insights/delivering -through-diversity.

10. "Who Invents IT? Women's Participation in Information Technology Patenting (2022 Update)," NCWIT.org, 2022, https:// ncwit.org/resource/ncwit-patenting-report-2022-update/.

11. Emily Chang, *Brotopia: Breaking Up the Boys' Club of Silicon Valley* (New York: Portfolio, 2018).

12. For a discussion on how people's assumptions about and definitions of success open the door to bias, see Lori Nishiura Mackenzie and Shelley J. Correll, "Two Powerful Ways Managers Can Curb Implicit Biases," hbr.org, October 1, 2018, https://hbr.org/2018/10 /two-powerful-ways-managers-can-curb-implicit-biases.

13. Joshua Wolf Shenk, "The End of 'Genius,'" *New York Times,* July 19, 2014, https://www.nytimes.com/2014/07/20/opinion/sunday/the -end-of-genius.html.

14. Walter Isaacson, in his book *The Innovators* (New York: Simon & Schuster, 2015), talks about the myth of the lone genius. His research illustrates that the so-called geniuses he covers are successful because they work collaboratively with others. The key to collaboration is communicating with each other.

15. "Girls, Share Your Horror Stories of Working in Tech," Reddit, https://www.reddit.com/r/cscareerquestions/comments/xf42k9/girls _share_your_horror_stories_of_working_in_tech/, accessed November 6, 2024.

Chapter 2

1. Marc de Jong, Laura Furstenthal, and Erik Roth, "What Is Innovation?," McKinsey, August 17, 2022, https://www.mckinsey.com /featured-insights/mckinsey-explainers/what-is-innovation.

2. Maria Popova, "Stephen Jay Gould on the Key to Creativity and the Power of Connecting the Dots," *Marginalian,* https://www .themarginalian.org/2013/05/23/uncommon-genius-stephen-jay-gould -connections-creativity/, accessed November 10, 2024.

3. Ed Catmull and Amy Wallace, *Creativity, Inc.: Overcoming the Unseen Forces That Stand in the Way of True Inspiration* (New York: Random House, 2014).

4. Charlan Jeanne Nemeth, "Managing Innovation: When Less Is More," *California Management Review* 40, no. 1 (1997): 59–74, https:// doi.org/10.2307/41165922.

5. "Netscape," Wikipedia, https://en.wikipedia.org/wiki/Netscape, accessed November 10, 2024.

6. Walter Isaacson, in his book *The Innovators* (New York: Simon & Schuster, 2015), talks about the myth of the lone genius.

7. Nemeth, "Managing Innovation: When Less Is More."

8. "Who Invents IT? Women's Participation in Information Technology Patenting (2022 update)," NCWIT.org, 2022, https://ncwit .org/resource/ncwit-patenting-report-2022-update/.

9. Gary P. Pisano, "The Hard Truth About Innovative Cultures," *Havard Business Review,* January–February 2019, https://hbr.org/2019 /01/the-hard-truth-about-innovative-cultures.

10. Pisano, "The Hard Truth About Innovative Cultures."

11. Catmull and Wallace, *Creativity, Inc.*

12. Clare Duffy, "From the Brink of Bankruptcy to a 1,300% Stock Gain: How This CEO Turned Around Her Company," CNN, March 27, 2020, https://www.cnn.com/2020/03/27/tech/lisa-su-amd-risk -takers/index.html.

13. Iain Martin and Richard Nieva, "Lisa Su Saved AMD. Now She Wants Nvidia's AI Crown," *Forbes*, February 21, 2024, https://www .forbes.com/sites/iainmartin/2023/05/31/lisa-su-saved-amd-now -she-wants-nvidias-ai-crown/.

14. Brian Amble, "Moving Goal Posts and Gender Discrimination," Management-Issues.com, July 1, 2005, https://www.management-issues .com/news/2297/moving-goal-posts-and-gender-discrimination/.

Chapter 3

1. Amy C. Edmondson and Per Hugander, "4 Steps to Boost Psychological Safety at Your Workplace," hbr.org, June 22, 2021, https:// hbr.org/2021/06/4-steps-to-boost-psychological-safety-at-your -workplace.

2. "Leading While Female: Prepare for Backlash," Association for Psychological Science, February 11, 2016, https://www .psychologicalscience.org/news/minds-business/leading-while -female-prepare-to-counter-the-backlash.html.

3. Susan Cain, *Quiet: The Power of Introverts in a World That Can't Stop Talking* (New York: Crown, 2012).

4. Edmondson and Hugander, "4 Steps to Boost Psychological Safety."

5. Erin Macke et al., "Assignments Are Critical Tools to Achieve Workplace Gender Equity," *MIT Sloan Management Review,* January 4, 2022, https://sloanreview.mit.edu/article/assignments-are-critical -tools-to-achieve-workplace-gender-equity/.

6. Joan C. Williams and Marina Multhaup, "For Women and Minorities to Get Ahead, Managers Must Assign Work Fairly," hbr.org, March 5, 2018, https://hbr.org/2018/03/for-women-and-minorities-to -get-ahead-managers-must-assign-work-fairly.

7. Ruchika T. Malhotra, "Women of Color Get Asked to Do More 'Office Housework.' Here's How They Can Say No," hbr.org, April 6, 2018, https://hbr.org/2018/04/women-of-color-get-asked-to-do-more -office-housework-heres-how-they-can-say-no.

Chapter 4

1. Kirsten Weir, "Feel Like a Fraud?," American Psychological Association, 2013, https://www.apa.org/gradpsych/2013/11/fraud; Bonnie Burton, "Imposter Syndrome Leaves Most Tech Workers Feeling Like a Fake," CNET, September 6, 2018, https://www.cnet.com /science/tech-employees-likely-to-suffer-from-impostor-syndrome/.

2. Stefan Wuchty, Benjamin F. Jones, and Brian Uzzi, "The Increasing Dominance of Teams in Production of Knowledge," *Science* 316, no. 5827 (2007): 1036–1039, doi: 10.1126/Science.1136099.

3. "Stereotype Threat," Perception Institute, https://perception .org/research/stereotype-threat/, accessed November 11, 2024.

4. Porter Braswell, "The Real Reason More Women and People of Color Suffer from Imposter Syndrome," *Fast Company*, March 21, 2023, https://www.fastcompany.com/90868279/imposter-syndrome-is-a -collective-burden-not-a-personal-problem.

5. Laura Guillen, "Is the Confidence Gap Between Men and Women a Myth?," hbr.org, March 26, 2018, https://hbr.org/2018/03 /is-the-confidence-gap-between-men-and-women-a-myth.

6. Alan Benson, Danielle Li, and Kelly Shue, "'Potential' and the Gender Promotion Gap," July 24, 2023, *Academy of Management* 2023, no. 1 (2023).

7. Alexis Krivkovich et al., "Women in the Workplace 2024: The 10th-Anniversary Report," McKinsey & Company, September 17, 2024, https://www.mckinsey.com/featured-insights/diversity-and-inclusion /women-in-the-workplace.

8. Nadra Nittle, "The Language of Gender Bias in Performance Reviews," Insights by Stanford Business, April 28, 2021, https://www .gsb.stanford.edu/insights/language-gender-bias-performance -reviews.

9. Sylvia Ann Hewlett, "Cracking the Code That Stalls People of Color," hbr.org, January 22, 2014, https://hbr.org/2014/01/cracking -the-code-that-stalls-multicultural-professionals.

10. W. Brad Johnson and David G. Smith, "Men, Stop Calling Yourselves Allies. Act Like One," hbr.org, August 5, 2022, https://hbr .org/2022/08/men-stop-calling-yourselves-allies-act-like-one.

11. Karen Catlin, *Better Allies: Everyday Actions to Create Inclusive, Engaging Workplaces* (Karen Catlin Consulting, 2019).

12. Janice Omadeke, "What's the Difference Between a Mentor and a Sponsor?," hbr.org, October 20, 2021, https://hbr.org/2021/10/whats -the-difference-between-a-mentor-and-a-sponsor.

13. Susan Fowler, "Reflecting on One Very, Very Strange Year at Uber," susanjfowler.com, February 19, 2017, https://www.susanjfowler .com/blog/2017/2/19/reflecting-on-one-very-strange-year-at-uber, accessed November 11, 2024.

Chapter 5

1. Back then the "W" stood for Women in Computing. Today the group has broadened its focus to all underrepresented groups and renamed itself CRA-WP, or the Committee on Widening Participation in Computing Research.

2. Cyril Bouquet, Jean-Louis Barsoux, and Michael Wade, "Bring Your Breakthrough Ideas to Life," *Harvard Business Review*, November–December 2018, https://hbr.org/2018/11/bring-your -breakthrough-ideas-to-life.

3. Lori Nishiura Mackenzie and Shelley J. Correll, "Two Powerful Ways Managers Can Curb Implicit Biases," hbr.org, October 1, 2018, https://hbr.org/2018/10/two-powerful-ways-managers-can-curb -implicit-biases.

4. David Rock, Heidi Grant, and Jacqui Grey, "Diverse Teams Feel Less Comfortable—and That's Why They Perform Better," hbr.org, September 22, 2016, https://hbr.org/2016/09/diverse-teams-feel-less -comfortable-and-thats-why-they-perform-better.

5. For more information, see Katie Wullert, Shannon Gilmartin, and Caroline Simard, "The Mistake Companies Make When They Use Data to Plan Diversity Efforts," hbr.org, April 16, 2019, https://hbr .org/2019/04/the-mistake-companies-make-when-they-use-data-to -plan-diversity-efforts.

Chapter 6

1. Walter Isaacson, in his book *The Innovators*, talks about the myth of the lone genius. His research illustrates that the so-called geniuses he covers are successful because they work collaboratively with others. The key to collaboration is communicating with each other.

2. Deborah James and Janice Drakich,"Understanding Gender Differences in Amount of Talk: A Critical Review of Research," in D. Tannen, ed., *Gender and Conversational Interaction* (New York: Oxford University Press, 1993); Alice Robb, "Women Get Interrupted More—Even by Other Women," *New Republic*, May 14, 2014, https://newrepublic.com/article/117757/gender-language-differences-women-get-interrupted-more.

3. Amy Gallo, "What Is Psychological Safety?," hbr.org, February 15, 2023, https://hbr.org/2023/02/what-is-psychological-safety.

4. Jennifer Robin and Michael Burchell, *No Excuses: How You Can Turn Any Workplace into a Great One* (San Francisco: Jossey Bass, 2013), 5–6.

5. Michael C. Bush, "9 High-Trust Leadership Behaviors Everyone Should Model," Great Place to Work, May 16, 2023, https://www.greatplacetowork.com/resources/blog/9high-trust-leadership-behaviors-everyone-should-model.

6. Sabina Nawaz, "What Stops People on Your Team from Leaving?," hbr.org, March 14, 2022, https://hbr.org/2022/03/what-stops-people-on-your-team-from-leaving.

7. For a thorough discussion of questions to ask during a stay interview, see Ava Martinez, "The Art of Asking the Right Questions—How to Conduct Stay Interviews," HR Digest, April 30, 2024, https://www.thehrdigest.com/the-art-of-asking-the-right-questions-how-to-conduct-stay-interviews/ and Darci Davis, "37 Best Questions to Ask Employees in Stay Interviews," Indeed, August 18, 2024, https://www.indeed.com/career-advice/interviewing/stay-interviews-questions.

8. Nawaz, "What Stops People on Your Team from Leaving?"

9. Leigh Honeywell, "Bingo and Beyond," *hypatia dot ca* (blog), September 23, 2015, https://hypatia.ca/2015/09/23/bingo-and-beyond/, accessed November 11, 2024.

10. Cathy O'Neil, "What Male Allies Should *Really* Be Doing," Mathbabe, October 10, 2014, https://mathbabe.org/2014/10/10/what-male-allies-should-really-be-doing/.

11. "Halo Effect," Psychology Today, https://www.psychologytoday.com/us/basics/halo-effect, accessed November 11, 2024.

12. Naia Toke, "The Horn Effect Bias: A Guide to Eliminating Hidden Biases," Diversity for Social Impact, March 17, 2023, https://diversity.social/horn-effect-bias/.

13. Patrick Healy, "Overcoming Confirmation Bias in the Workplace," *Business Insights* (blog), August 18, 2016, https://online.hbs.edu/blog/post/confirmation-bias-how-it-affects-your-organization-and-how-to-overcome-it.

14. Lily Jampol, Aneeta Rattan, and Elizabeth Baily Wolf, "Women Get 'Nicer' Feedback—and It Holds Them Back," hbr.org, January 25, 2023, https://hbr.org/2023/01/women-get-nicer-feedback-and-it -holds-them-back.

15. Elena Doldor, Madeleine Wyatt, and Jo Silvester, "Research: Men Get More Actionable Feedback Than Women," hbr.org, February 10, 2021, https://hbr.org/2021/02/research-men-get-more-actionable -feedback-than-women.

16. Shelley J. Correll et al., "Inside the Black Box of Organizational Life: The Gendered Language of Performance Assessment," *American Sociological Review* 85, no. 6 (2020): 1022–1050.

17. Deborah Ashton, "Does Race or Gender Matter More to Your Paycheck?," hbr.org, June 10, 2014, https://hbr.org/2014/06/does-race -or-gender-matter-more-to-your-paycheck.

18. Nadra Nittle, "The Language of Gender Bias in Performance Reviews," Insights by Stanford Business, April 28, 2021, https://www .gsb.stanford.edu/insights/language-gender-bias-performance -reviews.

Chapter 7

1. Julia Taylor Kennedy and Pooja Jain-Link, "What Does It Take to Build a Culture of Belonging?," hbr.org, June 21, 2021, https://hbr .org/2021/06/what-does-it-take-to-build-a-culture-of-belonging.

2. Jon Clifton, "The Power of Work Friends," hbr.org, October 7, 2022, https://hbr.org/2022/10/the-power-of-work-friends.

3. Sarah K. White, "Women in Tech Statistics: The Hard Truths of an Uphill Battle," CIO.com, March 8, 2024, https://www.cio.com /article/201905/women-in-tech-statistics-the-hard-truths-of-an -uphill-battle.html.

4. Elena Doldor, Madeleine Wyatt, and Jo Silvester, "Research: Men Get More Actionable Feedback Than Women," hbr.org, February 10, 2021, https://hbr.org/2021/02/research-men-get-more-actionable -feedback-than-women.

INDEX

ACKNOWLEDGMENTS

When I decided to write a book, I had no idea where this journey would take me, and I am eternally grateful for all the people who helped and encouraged me along the way. I find that the experience of joy and happiness, as well as of challenges, is always about the people around me who love and support me. They are what make it worth getting up in the morning. This book is not just my journey but our journey, and I am thankful for your part in it.

I owe a debt of gratitude to my book coach and editor, Genoveva Llosa. Her insightful partnership was not just helpful but transformative. In moments of overwhelm, her astute commentary altered both my approach and my perspective. She gently steered me and provided crucial feedback that, though at times tough to accept, was instrumental in shaping the book you hold today.

I am grateful to the entire Harvard Business Review Press staff, with a special acknowledgment to my editor there, Courtney Cashman. Her pivotal role in guiding the content of the book was instrumental. Courtney's thoughtful comments and feedback were crucial in helping me understand and manage the book creation process. I appreciate other members of the team including Jennifer Waring, Cheyenne Paterson, and Joshua Olejarz. I would also like to thank Julie Devoll, Felicia Sinusas, Alexandra Kephart, Sally Ashworth, Jon Shipley, Lindsey Dietrich, and Jordan Concannon for their help in marketing the book.

Thank you to Mia Nguyen for her many ideas and her help communicating them.

I am particularly grateful to the women who provided feedback on the first early draft. Giving them a copy of the manuscript felt like I was baring my soul to the outside world and exposing my guts. It was scary. Sally Ahnger, Mary Beth Westmoreland, Angela Tucci, Caroline Simard, Kathy Hill, and Audrey Van Belleghem, your feedback and encouragement were particularly valuable—and made a significant difference to the content of the finished manuscript.

This book is about people working in technology, and I am grateful to all the technologists and leaders who took the time to answer my questions, share their experiences, and provide the meaningful and thoughtful advice that I shared. My deepest thanks to (in alphabetical order) Aicha Evans, Al Zollar, Alan Eustace, Amanda Zimmermann, Ana Pinczuk, Ashley Conard, Ayna Agarwal, Blake Irving, Bob Nunn, Brianna Fugate, Bridget Frey, Caroline Simard, Christine Chiu, Colin Parris, Darby Dunn, Diane Bryant, Diane Greene, Ellora Israni, Emma Catlin, Erica Lockheimer, Françoise Brougher, Gaby Aguilera, Geetha Kannan, Hector Ruiz, Jennifer Chayes, Kevin Scott, Kim Warren, Li Fan, Marie Wieck, Mark Papermaster, Mary Lou Jepsen, Mike Schroepfer, Natalia Rodriguez, Nick Donofrio, Pam Kostka, Raquel Romano, Rebecca Parsons, Sameer Halepete, Sarah Loos, Shanna-Shaye Forbes, Shari Meggs, Stu Feldman, Thuan Pham, Tom Bradicich, Tybra Arthur, Tzumu Lin, Vanessa Farias, Vijay Anand, and an anonymous interview. Your stories are what made the book real. A special thank-you to Lisa Su for answering questions via email.

I appreciate the work of the Momentum Institute and its leadership, particularly Linda Sachs and Kate Lehman. Kaitlyn Stormes was immensely helpful in developing the survey instrument I used in the fall of 2021 and in guiding the analysis of the results. I am also grateful to Laura Palucki Blake, Jennifer Green, and Timothy Hussey from Harvey Mudd College and to Maria Klawe for our discussions of the survey responses from Harvey Mudd students. Maria provided me with friendship and sponsorship that goes back to the early days of the Grace Hopper Celebration and continues throughout my professional journey. She and I channel our mutual friend Anita Borg in all that we do. Our many hours together have included hikes in the mountains of the United States and Canada, where we solved all the world's problems. I value your friendship more than I can say.

I am deeply grateful to the people who I am closest to—my husband, William Scholtz, and my dear friends Abbie Layton and Katherine Dumont. All three of you not only make everything in life better but also make my journey more meaningful. Bill has always urged me to follow my passion and is my partner, lovingly and spiritually, in life. Abbie was the writer in our childhood and today remains a voice of love and well-being in my head. Katherine is the writer in our friendship, and she always reminds me of the importance to do this work.

My parents didn't get a chance to see this book, but all three of them, Hardin, Beverly, and June, live on through me. They taught me that I could do anything. My sisters, Denise, Sharon, Ann, Kathryn, and Carol, demonstrate what it means to have a family and are important to everything that I do. My brother Charlie isn't here in person anymore, but I hold him in my heart.

Many friends listened to me as I decided on so many aspects of this book, including Chris Wellens, Sheryl Young, Amy Pearl, Susan Owicki, and Sally Ahnger. There were many walks on the beach of Santa Cruz and in the mountains nearby that helped feed my soul and keep me going. There were many Zoom calls over the years that kept our connection alive. James Beck and

I walked miles on Bay Area trails and talked about the future. Denise Brosseau provided me with ideas, connections, feedback, and friendship. Every time I wondered what it looked like to write a book, Denise showed me the way.

Many people helped in the early days. Emily Chang made several important suggestions early on and was inspirational in her own book journey as I decided to write this book. Jennifer Chayes offered me encouragement to write the book. Valerie Taylor was always supportive, was available for conversations about the importance of all kinds of diversity, and always found a way to discuss what was important in a book like this. Richard Ladner challenged me to consider what it means to include people with disabilities.

There are many people who I worked with over the years who are part of this manuscript even if they don't realize it. From the Anita Borg days, Jody Mahoney, Elizabeth Ames, Audrey Van Belleghem, Mary Kempski, Farideh Eshagh, Theresa Matacia, Carol Gustaveson, Laurie Greer, Stuti Badoni, Leslie Wilkerson, and Roshni Kasad helped inform many of the ideas present in this book. Thank you to Greg Papadopoulos and Maria encouraging me to take on the role of CEO of the Anita Borg Institute. It changed my life.

At NCWIT, Lucy Sanders, Bobby Schnabel, and I met every week for many years, and our thoughtful conversations contributed to the ideas explored in his book.

I appreciate the people who continue to make a difference in the future through their organizations. They are my inspiration for making a difference. These include Tess Posner, Emily Reid, Olga Russakovsky, Fei-Fei Li, Lauren Pimpare, Huma Hamid, Wenchi Yu, Pratima Gluckman, Radhika Rangarajan, Kathy Renzetti, Thea Sahr, Dwana Frankilin-Davis, and Jeff Boudro. Your work impacts the lives of so many, including a number of those featured in this book.

In my career, there were many people who were instrumental in my journey. I'd like to thank Cindy Lain, Bob Nunn, Forest Baskett, Curtis Abbott, Carol Realini, Shelly Begun, Bill Unger, John East, Rich Mora, Jim Davis, Penny Herscher, Dana How, Sifuei Ku, Sam Beal, Kirk Ross, Tara Anderson, Jeff Schlageter, Tom Todd, Ahmad Ghaemmaghami, Homayoun Shahri, Chung Chan, and Rebecca Norlander. My dear friend Carver Mead played an instrumental role throughout my professional career. His focus on science lives on in my head and my heart every day.

Thank you to Mary Jane Irwin and Fran Berman, who encouraged Anita Borg and me to create the Grace Hopper Celebration when they were the cochairs of CRA-W, the committee on women from CRA where the ideas of the Grace Hopper Celebration were born. Their passion for women having a voice in the leadership of technology inspired me and changed the world.

Thank you to those who were part of my early days in computing, when we still had big tape drives and large computers. Vernon Dwire, thank you for reconnecting with me and reminiscing about our early days of tech. I miss you. Mary Braun, thank you for being my early technical role model. I would also like to acknowledge Mary Gray for our early technology roots and the many backcountry trips we shared.

ABOUT THE AUTHOR

TELLE WHITNEY is a senior executive leader and a recognized expert and advocate for diversity, inclusion, and women in technology. She has over twenty years of leadership experience and is a sought-after speaker on diversity topics. Telle has been called "a pioneer for the promotion of women technologists" and was named one of *Fast Company*'s Most Influential Women in Technology.

She served as CEO of the Anita Borg Institute from 2002 to 2017 and cofounded the Grace Hopper Celebration of Women in Computing conference with Anita Borg in 1994. She transformed the institute into a recognized world leader for women and technology. The Grace Hopper Celebration—which attracted five hundred attendees in 1994—is the world's largest annual gathering of women technologists, attended by more than thirty thousand of them in 2023. Telle is also the cofounder of the National Center for Women and Information Technology. She serves on many boards and advisory councils, including the board of AI4All, a nonprofit focused on educating the next generation of AI technologists, thinkers, and leaders, and the board of the Center for Minorities and People with Disabilities in Information Technology.

Prior to joining the Anita Borg Institute, Telle was vice president of engineering for Malleable Technologies, a startup, where she led the creation and scale-up of the company's engineering function and turned the founder's initial idea into a reality.

Her expertise—creating workplaces where diverse groups of technologists can achieve their highest personal potential while helping to foster innovation and profitability for their employers—has elevated her position as an oft-quoted media source. Telle's work has been mentioned in national media, including CNBC, *Time*, *Forbes*, and NPR, and she has written for *Fortune*, TechCrunch, and *Computer* magazine. She's been featured or quoted in *Brotopia: Breaking Up the Boys' Club of Silicon Valley*, by Emily Chang, and *Good Guys: How Men Can Be Better Allies for Women in the Workplace*, by David G. Smith and W. Brad Johnson. Her story was included in *Lessons Learned: Stories from Women Leaders in STEM*, edited by Deborah M. Shlian; *Healing Leadership: How to Lead, Love, and Thrive in Business and Life*, by Ginny A. Baro; *Dear Chairwoman: Letters from Today's Trailblazing Women Board Leaders to the Fearless Directors of Tomorrow*, by Rika Nakazawa; *Women in Microelectronics*, edited by Alice Cline Parker and Leda Lunardi; *Rendering History: The Women of ACM-W*, edited by Gloria Childress Townsend; and *Nevertheless, She Persisted: True Stories of Women Leaders in Tech*, by Pratima Rao Gluckman.

Telle has won numerous awards, including the Association for Computing Machinery's Distinguished Service Award, an honorary membership from the Institute of Electrical and Electronics Engineers, and an honorary degree from Carnegie Mellon University. She was elected to the National Academy of Engineering in 2022. She holds a PhD and an MS in computer science from the California Institute of Technology and a BS in computer science from the University of Utah.